modern nationalities

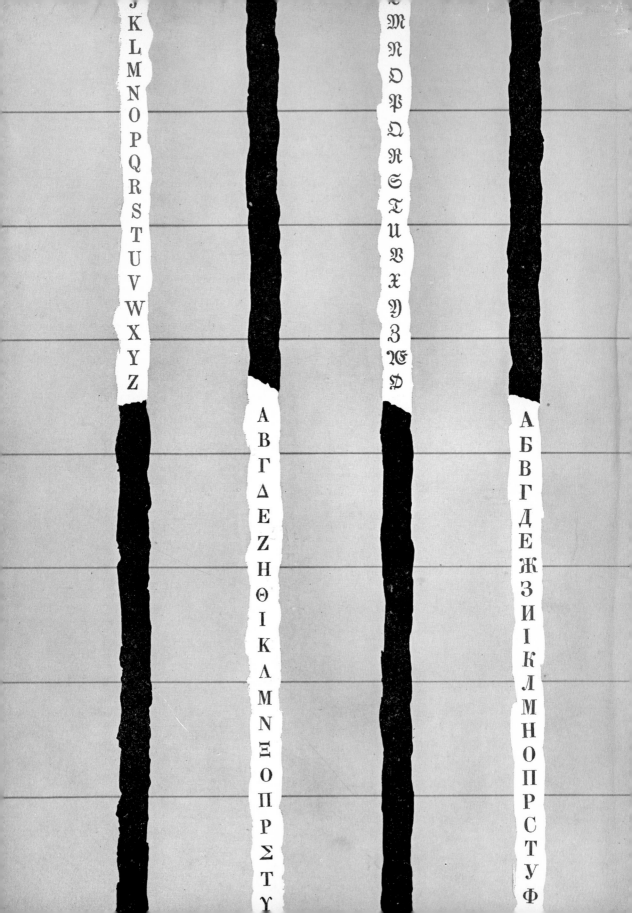

THE UNIVERSITY OF ILLINOIS PRESS IN URBANA · 1952

Modern Nationalities

a sociological study   BY FLORIAN ZNANIECKI

to all my former students
who, coming from twenty-eight different nationalities,
cooperated with me in a common search for knowledge.

contents

preface

This is a summary of the results of a sociological study which I began thirty-five years ago. It is based mostly on a comparative analysis of numerous works of historians, biographers, ideologists, men of letters, sociologists, and observers of social life in many countries, and includes some observations of my own and my assistants. Many of my students made valuable contributions.[1] An earlier, much shorter preliminary outline, written for a course I gave at the University of Illinois, was published in Spanish translation.[2]

The fundamental idea—that a solidary human collectivity of hundreds of thousands, even millions, of people who share the same culture can exist for a long time without a common political government—is not new. Long ago religious thinkers realized that people who share the same religion can be socially united while living in several separate states. Certain social philosophers in the middle of the eighteenth century applied this idea to people who share the same secular or national culture, even when they are not politically united. The conception of these philosophers, however, was at first an ideal rather than a theory based on factual evidence, and it evidently conflicted with the predominant doctrine of political scientists that the only effective social unity is that of an organized state, as well as with the theory of those sociologists who assumed that the state, though not sufficient, is indispensable for the existence of a solidary, organized, modern society.

This sociological theory seemed doubtful to me, in view of my own experiences as a participant in social life. I was born and brought up in Poland at a time when that country was divided into three territories. The territory in which I lived, although inhabited by Poles, was included in the Russian Empire and subjected to complete control of the Tsarist government; while the other two territories, also inhabited by Poles, were parts of Prussia and Austria. For more than a century,

1. Quite a few of the contributions made during the last six years are mentioned in footnotes. Earlier contributions, unfortunately, are not available.

2. Florian Znaniecki, *Las Sociedades de Cultura Nacional y Sus Relaciones*, Jornadas 24, El Colegio de México, Centro de Estudios Sociales, 1944.

there was no united Polish state and no common Polish government. Yet this division did not prevent the Poles from maintaining and developing cooperatively a common Polish culture and an active solidarity which cut across the political boundaries, in spite of many obstructions imposed by the three ruling governments. And when at the Treaty of Versailles, Poland was finally recognized as an independent state, it took only a few years to organize a new Polish state.

Thus, the history of the Poles from the partition of Poland in 1795 up to 1919 not only seemed to disprove the doctrine that a common state is indispensable for social unity, but also suggested that the idea of those social philosophers who considered a common national culture as a more lasting and influential bond of social solidarity than a common government might prove to be a scientifically valid theory.

As a matter of fact, many Polish historians, ethnologists, and sociologists accepted it. They used the term *narod* to denote a socially solidary collectivity united by a common national culture. This term has no equivalent in English, although the word *nationality* approximates its meaning. They carried on numerous studies, mostly (though not exclusively) of the Polish nationality, the various active manifestations of its solidarity, and its relationships with other nationalities with which it was in contact. Probably more books and articles dealing with nationality problems have been published in Polish than in any other language.[3]

3. See, e.g., Eileen Markley Znaniecki, "Polish Sociology," *Twentieth Century Sociology*, eds. Georges Gurvitch and Wilbert E. Moore (New York: Philosophical Library, 1945); K. Symonolewicz, "The Studies in Nationality and Nationalism in Poland between the two Wars (1918-39)," *Bulletin of the Polish Institute of Arts and Sciences in America*, Vol. 2.

But, however suggestive the Polish case, the theory had to be tested by comparative study of other cases. And since it implied that a solidary nationality, to be active, had to have some social organization, distinct from the political organization of the state, in each particular case it was essential to discover whether such an organization existed.

Italy and Germany furnished two famous instances of the development of a common culture and social solidarity which preceded and conditioned the political unification of people divided into separate, often conflicting, states. In other instances, people who shared a distinct culture, but were included in a state dominated by people with a different culture, like the Poles, preserved their social solidarity and were enabled eventually, with some outside help, to form an independent state of their own, e.g., the Greeks, the Serbs, the Czechs, and the Irish.

I surveyed numerous other nationalities with distinctive cultures and found that every one of them had some degree of active solidarity and a specific social organization irreducible to political structures. Only a small part of my factual evidence can be included in this brief summary. Of course, my survey was necessarily only a preliminary, superficial one. It would take many sociologists a long time to carry on adequate research on a world-wide scale.

Nonetheless, the conclusion seems justified that this kind of organized social unity is steadily growing and gaining influence throughout the world. Unfortunately it is still underestimated by many social scientists and especially by statesmen. For any political plans which do not take it fully into consideration are bound to result in failure.

introduction

During the last fifty years, many historians, political scientists, social psychologists, and sociologists have investigated a trend in the modern world which has proved to be a powerful factor for both social solidarity and social conflict and which they call "nationalism." Numerous works have been published dealing with this subject.[1] The most important and best known are Carlton J. H. Hayes's *The Historical Evolution of Modern Nationalism* (New York: R. R. Smith, 1931) and Hans Kohn's *The Idea of Nationalism* (New York: Macmillan, 1944). Both are primarily concerned with various conceptions of national solidarity formulated by ideologists and their influence upon social life.[2]

The term "nationalism," however, is difficult to define.[3] It is derived from the word "nation" and consequently suggests a solidarity of the people who compose the nation. But, in the various languages in which it is used, "nation" has several different meanings. In English, it usually means the totality of citizens of a sovereign state. This is the sense in which legal and political thinkers have used it, e.g., in coining the terms "The League of Nations" and "The United Nations." But even in England it is often used in a different sense; thus, the Welsh call themselves a "nation," although Wales is not a sovereign state. French thinkers, though often using the term "nation" with a political connotation, nevertheless give it a more inclusive meaning than the English.[4] On the other hand, most German thinkers distinguish between *Nation* and *Staat*. In view of this terminological confusion the editors of several encyclopedias have omitted the term "nation" altogether.[5] We shall follow their example and never use it here.

Most investigators of modern nationalism now prefer the term "nationality" or its equivalent in another language. Although certain legislators make this term synonymous with citizenship in a sovereign state, this meaning can be ignored

1. Cf. Koppel S. Pinson, *A Bibliographical Introduction to Nationalism* (New York: Columbia University Press, 1935). So far as we know, no such bibliography of later works has yet been compounded.

2. The collective work *Nationalism* (Royal Institute of International Affairs, Oxford University Press, 1939) is mainly devoted to its political aspects.

3. Some authors implicitly assume or explicitly state that it is "not capable of scientific definition." Cf. H. L. Featherstone, *A Century of Nationalism* (New York: T. Nelson and Sons, 1939), p. 10. We shall postpone its definition till later (Chapter One, Sec. 3).

4. Scientifically the most exact and consistent use of this term is in *La Nation* by J. T. Delos, 2 vols. (Montreal, 1944).

5. *International Encyclopedia; Encyclopedia of the Social Sciences; Encyclopaedia Britannica; Handwörterbuch der Staatswissenschaften.*

6. This legal meaning is well exemplified by Édouard Bourbousson, *Traité général de la nationalité* (Paris, 1931). It includes three parts: "Du statut de la femme mariée"; "De la naturalisation"; "De la perte de la nationalité."

7. See, e.g., Arnold J. Toynbee, *Nationality and the War* (New York: Dutton, 1915); Leon Dominian, *The Frontiers of Language and Nationality in Europe* (New York: Holt, 1917); Israel Zangwill, *The Principle of Nationalities* (New York: Macmillan, 1917); Bertrand Auerbach, *Les Races et les Nationalités en Autriche-Hongrie* (Paris, 1917); René Johannet, *Le Principe des nationalités* (Paris, 1918); Comte Nicolas de Borsh, *Le Principe des nationalités et la question Lithuanienne* (Louvain, 1925).

by investigators as scientifically irrelevant.[6] As generally conceived by social scientists, "nationality" means a collectivity of people with certain common and distinctive cultural characteristics (language, customs, historical traditions, etc.), sometimes also "racial" traits and a definite geographic location. The study of such collectivities is, of course, very old; it goes back to classical antiquity (Strabo, even Herodotus) and was fully revived in the eighteenth century by European ethnologists. For instance, Herder, who as a philosopher of history is considered one of the most important nationalistic ideologists, was also one of the initiators and promoters of German ethnological research. The term "nationality," however, seems to have been introduced only in the second half of the nineteenth century. It was widely applied during the first quarter of this century in connection with the well-known political problem of reconciling the sovereignty of states with the autonomy of ethnic groups.[7] The problem was primarily practical; but some attempts were made to develop an objective theory of nationality. Methodically the most thorough and promising of these attempts was started by the Belgian ethnologist and sociologist Arnold Van Gennep, under the title *Traité comparatif des nationalités*. It was planned as three volumes: "I, Les Éléments exterieurs de la nationalité; II, La Formation des nationalités; III, La Vie des nationalités." Unfortunately, the author died soon after the first volume was published (Paris, 1922), and nobody has continued his work.

Most investigators of nationalism are well aware that nationalism as a social force requires not only the existence of collectivities which can be defined and circumscribed by certain ethnological criteria, but also the conscious and active solidarity of the people who compose such collectivities. A distinction has often been made between objective and subjective factors. Objective factors, such as language, customs, race, religion, territory, citizenship in a state, are considered to be easily observable and definable, though theorists disagree as to their

xiv

relative importance. Subjective factors, by their very definition, have to be investigated psychologically. However, they cannot be reduced to individual psychology, and consequently students of nationalities have used various conceptions of *collective psychology* to cover such subjective factors. These conceptions were derived from theories developed toward the end of the nineteenth century and at the beginning of the twentieth century: in Germany, where earlier, rather vague, doctrines of "Volksgeist" and "Volksseele" were systematized by Wundt in his *Völkerpsychologie;* in France, by Le Bon and partly by Fouillée; in England and America by McDougall and others. This psychological approach is found in such works as W. B. Pillsbury, *The Psychology of Nationality and Internationalism* (New York: Appleton, 1919) and Walter Sulzbach, *National Consciousness* (Washington, D.C.: Am. Council on Public Affairs, 1943). It has been most fully developed by Frederick Otto Hertz, *Nationality in History and Politics; a Study of the Psychology and Sociology of National Sentiment and Character* (London, 1945).[8]

This literature on nationality and nationalism contains much valuable material, but leaves two fundamental problems unsolved or inadequately solved. One of these problems is historical. Why did nationalism emerge so late in human history? Even Hans Kohn, who tries to trace the origin of the idea of nationalism back to Hebrew and Greek civilization, states that "nationalism as we understand it is not older than the second half of the eighteenth century" (*The Idea of Nationalism,* p. 3). We shall try to show that it evolved somewhat earlier and that there was an analogous evolution in classical antiquity, which eventually stopped—though this is a minor matter. In any case, it first developed fully in modern Europe, later slowly and gradually expanded to America and Asia, and now is beginning in some parts of Africa. Does this indicate some important *new* development in the Western world during this period? It could not have been a new type of political

8. See particularly pp. 14-51, where Hertz formulates his basic principles.

organization, for nationalism flourished under various political regimes. Some theorists try to explain it by the development of modern technology, which undoubtedly facilitated the growth and expansion of nationalism; but there is no significant correlation between the two. Indeed, as we shall see, one of the results of the industrial revolution is a recent social trend which conflicts with nationalism. The problem can be solved only in the light of a general history of culture.

The second problem is sociological. Since nationalism is recognized as a very influential social force, of which modern nationalities are the bearers, this means that a nationality is more than a collectivity of people *psychologically* united by common interests and aims. It must be, at least in some degree, *socially* organized. For one of the best-known results of sociological research is the discovery that organized groups are more influential, more powerful socially, than unorganized aggregates or masses of people. Now, students of nationalities have usually followed the example of political scientists and assumed that only the modern state, with a highly complex, inclusive, and well-integrated organization which gives it a monopoly of physical force, can actively realize nationalistic aims. They consequently have ignored the existence or at least underestimated the social influences of numerous and diverse nationalistic groups which are not included in the formal political structure of the state. We shall, therefore, devote much of our attention to the study of these groups.

one

National culture as

a relatively new type of culture

What does the term "culture" mean?

1. Thirty-five years ago I tried to develop such a theory; see *Cultural Reality* (Chicago: University of Chicago Press, 1919). Probably the most inclusive of all these theories is that of Pitirim Sorokin; cf. his *Social and Cultural Dynamics*, 4 vols. (New York: American Book, 1937-41).

Thinkers have formulated various conceptions of culture and various, often conflicting, theories of the relationship between culture and nature.[1] In order not to become involved here in controversial issues, we shall simply apply the concept of culture to those diverse kinds of empirical phenomena which anthropologists, folklorists, historians, and archeologists designate by this term. A comparative survey of their works indicates that what they call "culture" includes: (1) all the products of human actions; and (2) all those actions which human agents learn to perform from other human agents.

1. Products of human actions are usually subdivided by investigators into two classes: material and nonmaterial. The latter are sometimes called "spiritual," but we prefer to call them "ideational."

Material products are located in space, are fully accessible to sensory experience, and are used by men in physical activities. They include all kinds of tools and machines, food and drink when prepared for consumption, clothes, buildings, furniture, boats, carriages, roads, products of agriculture, horticulture, animal husbandry, etc. Obviously, all material products are also natural objects and can be observed and investigated as such. They are components of culture if and insofar as they owe their existence to purposive human activities. Plants growing in a cultivated field from seeds selected and sown by a farmer are in this sense cultural products, as distinct from wild plants growing independently of human activities.

Ideational products, as distinct from material products, cannot be located in space and are used not in physical, but in mental activities. Here belong all the products of imagination: mythical beings and events, such as totemic ancestors, Greek, Roman, or Hindu gods, angels and devils, the numerous and diverse stories of creation; half-mythical, half-fictitious beings and events, such as Odysseus and his travels or heroes and

2

their adventures, as presented in Greek tragedies; purely fictional beings and events, as described in literature. Another well-known category of ideational products is that of philosophic and scientific ideas and theories. Very important for students of culture are standards of values and norms of conduct—moral, political, technological, aesthetic, logical, etc.—with which human agents are supposed to conform, and all kinds of ideals expected to be realized in the future. Also important, especially from the sociological and sociopsychological point of view, are the various conceptions which individuals have of other individuals, of their own selves or egos, and of the social groups to which they belong, as well as of other groups to which they do not belong. In this class of ideational products we must also include language; for language is composed of words which have meanings, and the meaning of a word is an ideational, not a material, phenomenon. It is true that we can locate the sounds emitted by an individual in pronouncing a word, or the written or printed signs which symbolize this word in a manuscript or book, but the word itself with its meaning cannot be located in any particular place; yet it is the same word wherever spoken, written, or printed.

The same may be said of a poem or a musical composition. The poem can be read or declaimed, the musical composition played on the same day in places separated by thousands of miles; yet it remains always the same cultural product. Its identity is due to its aesthetic form and meaning, which make it emotionally and intellectually valuable to all who understand it, wherever they are located at the time they read, play, or hear it.

There is, however, an intermediary type of cultural product, which is material in the sense that it is located in space and yet has also an ideational significance. This type includes the works of painters, sculptors, and architects. Their artistic structure is meaningful to all who have seen and appreciated

3

it, because it does influence their experiences, feelings, and ideas.

This distinction between material and ideational cultural products is significant for our present problem. A product of material culture destined for physical use is intended to be used only by a limited number of individuals; whereas the number of people who can use an ideational product—worship the same deity, accept the same moral standard or norm, reproduce or admire the same piece of literature or of music, speak the same language—is not limited. Furthermore, while products of material culture become sooner or later destroyed by being used, products of ideational culture, on the contrary, become perpetuated and developed by being used; only if they cease to be used do they lose their significance and eventually disappear. Consequently, ideational culture constitutes a more influential and more lasting bond of social solidarity than material culture.

2. When we include within the domain of culture only those actions which human agents learn to perform from other human agents, we are aware that it is sometimes difficult to ascertain how much learning is needed for certain actions to be performed; for many actions originate in innate biopsychological drives, and some of these may be only slightly modified under social influences. There is no such difficulty so far as actions dealing with ideational products are concerned. The use of language—speaking, understanding other people's speech, writing, reading—requires learning. So does the understanding and use of other ideational products—religion, literature, music, moral ideology, philosophy, science. And, manifestly, no one can create new ideational products unless he has first learned to understand such products created by others.

In the realm of material culture, productive human actions have also to be learned, for material techniques have developed slowly and gradually in the course of history, and every collectivity possessed definite standards and norms with which producers are supposed to conform. To use a term coined by

4

cultural anthropologists, technically productive actions are "culturally patterned," and individuals who perform them are taught how to follow the patterns. This is most obvious when the technical actions are performed collectively, as in a factory, for then every individual must learn how to cooperate with others. Many material products, however, can be used for the satisfaction of biological needs without special learning; animals do not need to be taught how to eat. But even such a use of material products by men is often culturally patterned; thus, in many collectivities eating specific dishes or drinking wine is supposed to follow certain rules of etiquette.

The same distinction applies to social actions, i.e., those which deal with human individuals or groups. Just like similar actions of animals, sexual intercourse, actions of a mother protecting or feeding her infant, juvenile free-for-alls can be carried on with little or no learning. Most social actions, however, are supposed to conform with definite norms—customary, moral, legal—and, when they do, this means that the agent has been taught by others to act as these norms require; that is, to follow a cultural pattern which others consider right.

Obviously, while any particular action is performed at a particular time by an individual or group located at that time in a particular place, the cultural pattern which it follows can spread indefinitely and last indefinitely; thousands, even millions, of agents can repeatedly perform for many years similarly patterned technical actions, religious actions, and social actions.

What is a culture?

Although quite a few works have been written about culture in general, trying to trace its total evolution from prehistoric times to the modern period, the great majority of cultural scientists have been investigating *particular cultures* as concrete combinations of numerous and diverse cultural products and patterns. To mention some familiar examples: cultural anthropologists have studied Navaho culture, Zuñi culture, Kwakiutl culture in North America, the culture of Trobriand islanders, of Andamanese islanders, Arunta culture in Australia, many diverse cultures in Central and Southern Africa. Ethnologists and folklorists have studied numerous local cultures in rural and small-town communities of Europe and found that communities within a certain region are more or less similar culturally and differ more or less from communities in other regions. Such regions with different cultures can be distinguished, e.g., Brittany, Normandy, Auvergne, Touraine in France; Devon, Cornwall, Kent in England; Thuringia, Hanover, East Prussia in Germany; Mazovia, Silesia, Kujavia in Poland; Piedmont, Tuscany, Campagna in Italy. Historians have studied such famous cultures (sometimes called "civilizations") as Egyptian, Sumerian, Greek, Roman, Arab, Hindu, Chinese, French, German, Italian.

Now, each of these cultures has been maintained in existence for a long historical period by people belonging to a particular collectivity which has lasted for generations; and each contains certain basic ideational and material components—language, a set of religious beliefs and practices, certain conceptions of nature and man, mores regulating human relationships, some poetry, music and plastic arts, products of material culture essential for the satisfaction of biological needs, and culturally patterned ways of producing and using them. But these specific components differ considerably.

Attempts have been made to explain this diversity of cultures by natural causes—racial differences within the human genus or differences in geographic environment. The former have been completely, the latter partly, invalidated. Valid explanation must be sought in the history of the relationships between these cultures and of the collectivities which maintain them. For no culture can exist without a solidary, more or less

6

organized, collectivity whose members cooperate in producing and maintaining common cultural values and patterns of actions, and transmit these values and patterns from generation to generation. On the other hand, no solidary human collectivity can exist unless its members are united by common cultural values (primarily common ideational values), and it cannot be organized unless the actions of its members follow definite cultural patterns. Inasmuch as solidary human collectivities have always been limited in size and socially separated (if not isolated) from other collectivities, each of them has tended to perpetuate a distinctive common culture of its own.

Of course, cultures do not remain changeless; in the course of their duration some old values and patterns disappear, new values and patterns are introduced, either by original initiative of their participants or by importation from other cultures, though we often find considerable resistance to such innovations. And, what is even more important from the point of view of our present problem, new cultures can develop by a gradual process of creative growth.

Both the solidarity of the collectivity which maintains a culture and the perpetuation of this culture depend upon symbolic communication between those who participate in it. Cultures can be classified, and have been classified, according to the way in which cultural values, especially ideational values, and patterns of actions are consciously shared by contemporary participants and transmitted from generation to generation. The fundamental difference is between cultures which are shared and transmitted only by oral communication and those in which writing is used.

The importance of this difference is manifest. For the conscious spread of any product of ideational culture or any cultural pattern of action from individual to individual by word of mouth depends upon face-to-face contacts. To share and maintain in this way such a cultural complex as a language, with its thousands of words whose pronunciation, meaning, and combination into sentences follow phonetical, semantical, and grammatical rules considered binding for all, there must be many prolonged direct contacts among the people who use the language. This means that these people must live within a limited area where mobility is relatively easy; otherwise, it would be very difficult to maintain a common language. This is shown by the great diversity of spoken languages and dialects in mountainous territories; for instance, during the nineteenth century, linguists found several hundred languages and dialects within the territory of the Caucasus. By contrast, a written language can spread indefinitely and be shared by millions of people living in distant areas.

The same may be said about religion. Religion consists not so much in myths as in regular active cultus. In order to share religious beliefs and practices which can be only orally communicated, believers must meet periodically. Thus, maintenance of the totemic religions of Australian tribes was possible only because each tribe congregated every year; and the religious cultus of a Pueblo Indian group is highly developed, continuous, and integrated, because the group lives closely together. Whereas a religion with its dogmas and norms of cultus formulated in written documents can be shared not only by those—wherever they live—who read these documents and accept these dogmas and norms (mostly priests), but also by all those to whom the priests communicate orally the content of the documents and whose beliefs and actions they guide and control.

Of course, some of the cultural values and patterns communicated orally become diffused, i.e., spread from collectivity to collectivity through travels and other contacts; but this is a slow process, and in its course these values and patterns are apt to change.

Equally obvious and important is the difference between the perpetuation of a culture through oral communication and its perpetuation through writing. The duration of a culture orally transmitted from generation to generation depends on the memory of the older generation and its control over the younger generation. Such a culture may last, indeed, through many generations, though it inevitably undergoes some changes; but it can also, and sometimes does, disappear in the course of two or three generations. For whatever is forgotten by the older generation or neglected by the younger is lost forever.

Whereas documents, if preserved or copied, can be read and reread indefinitely, centuries after they were originally written. This means that the products of ideational culture created in a distant past can be used again and again for new cultural products. Therefore, a culture transmitted by writing can grow much more rapidly and become much richer than a culture orally transmitted. Consider, for instance, the growth of the many and divergent Christian theological and ethical doctrines from the second century to this day, or the new cultural developments during and after the Renaissance based on the rediscovery of partly forgotten works of Greek and Roman philosophers, political theorists, poets, and historians.

Some anthropologists who investigate collectivities in which only spoken language is used have introduced the term *preliterate* or *nonliterate* to distinguish them from those in which a written language has developed. These English terms, however, refer mainly to the *people* who do not know how to write and read, rather than to their *cultures;* and it is difficult to find equivalents for them in other languages.[2] Consequently, we have coined the term *traditional cultures* to denote those in which the continuous duration of cultural values and patterns of actions is due to their direct transmission from generation to generation by spoken language.

In contrast with them, we shall call *literary cultures* those which owe their continued existence to literary works, because these works contain symbolic descriptions of ideational values on which social solidarity is based and symbolic expression of standards and norms by which the actions of participants are

2. Dr. Vicente Herrero, who translated the earlier outline of this study into Spanish, first attracted my attention to the limitation of these terms.

supposed to be guided. In other words, a *literary culture* is one of which literature (in the widest sense of the term) is the most influential component.

Two types of traditional culture can be and have been distinguished by investigators. Most of those which cultural anthropologists study are relatively independent, because the collectivities which maintain them have—or have had until recent times—a considerable degree of social autonomy, insofar as they are not yet incorporated into powerful modern political societies. Here belong, for instance, quite a few Australian natives, a few Melanesian and Polynesian collectivities, ethnic groups in central Sumatra and Borneo, those Indians of North America who are allowed to preserve their organization and their culture, Indians in central Brazil, and numerous ethnic groups in Central Africa. The prevalent, almost universal, characteristic of these collectivities is that they constitute tribes. A tribe is a group designated by a distinct name, united by a belief in common ancestors from whom its culture was originally derived, and possessing some degree of social integration. We shall consequently call the culture maintained by such groups *tribal*.

On the other hand, the traditional rural and small-town cultures which ethnologists, especially Europeans, have been studying for the last century and a half are maintained by collectivities which have lost their independence; they live in areas which fall within the territory belonging to an organized state and are subjected to the control of the government of this state. We shall call them *folk cultures,* following investigators who use the term "folklore" to designate distinct traits of these cultures. Many ethnologists used to consider all folk cultures as survivals of old tribal cultures. This may be true of some regional traditional cultures found in Great Britain, Germany, Poland, and Russia, but not in France, where Latin culture was superimposed upon the tribal cultures of ancient Gaul. Moreover, the history of folk cultures shows that almost all of

10

them include components which were borrowed in a more or less distant past from literary cultures, modified in adaptation to pre-existing traditional cultures, and hereafter orally transmitted.

A comparative survey of literary cultures indicates that they differ according to the content and meaning of the literary works on which their unity and continuity depend. Where the dominant components are *sacred* books of presumably divine origin, the culture is basically different from cultures in which *secular* literature, without claim to divine origin, predominates. We shall call the first type of literary culture *religious;* the second, *national.* The first type is exemplified by the Hindu culture, based upon the Upanishads and the Veddas; by Jewish culture, based upon the Torah and the Talmud; by Islamic culture, based upon the Koran; and by various Christian cultures—Roman Catholic, Greek Orthodox, Lutheran, Calvinist—all based upon the Old and the New Testaments, though somewhat differently interpreted.

The adjective "national" has already been applied to such modern cultures as the Italian, the French, the English, the German; it may be extended also to ancient Greek culture of the classical and the Hellenistic periods, and to Latin culture from the second century B.C. to the Christianization of Western Europe, when Latin became a religious rather than a secular language. Of course, no sharp dividing line can be drawn between the two types of literary cultures; national cultures may contain some religious components, and religious cultures may incorporate some components of national culture. In Chinese literary culture, religious ideologies and the secular ideology of Confucianism coexisted for two thousand years. Nevertheless, the distinction is important, both from the historical and from the sociological point of view.

It is especially important in recent times, when new national cultures are evolving from older religious cultures. Thus, we observe a new, rapidly developing Jewish national culture,

11

mainly rooted in the old religious culture, but partly also in the folk cultures which grew up in various European countries.[3] Likewise, a national culture in India has begun to evolve out of religious Hinduism.[4] While the Islamic religious culture initiated by the Arabs is shared by peoples with widely different secular cultures, a new national Arabic culture is growing which only Arabs share.[5]

Since writing was probably invented everywhere by priests, religious cultures developed long before national cultures began to emerge. Writing was first used to stabilize and perpetuate conceptions of mythical beings and events, as well as standards and norms regulating religious cultus and eventually also all human actions judged to be important for the community of the faithful. A literary work may be held "sacred," if the knowledge it contains is considered absolutely true and the principles of conduct formulated by its authors absolutely valid; to doubt the truth of its knowledge or to question the validity of its principles would be profanation of its sacredness.

Moreover, sacred books, as foundations of religious cultures, are supposed to solve all human problems, ideational and practical. But, as time goes on and new problems emerge, application of the truths and principles expressed in a sacred book is not always clear or easy. The book must be interpreted by those who understand it fully for the benefit of those who lack this understanding. Also, any criticisms by unbelievers must be invalidated. Consequently, works by commentators, interpreters, defenders of the faith gradually agglomerate. For instance, thousands of works on Christian theology have accumulated in the course of centuries, written by the early "fathers of the Church," medieval Catholic thinkers, and later Protestant theologians.

In collectivities where a sacred literature is universally accepted as absolutely valid, all ideational culture and often also many actions producing and using material values acquire a religious significance. The moral standards and norms which

3. Rich materials on this development are contained in the numerous historical works concerning Jewish communities in Europe and, more recently, in America, and in those concerning the growth of Jewish literature in Hebrew and in Yiddish, from the middle of the nineteenth century on. Cf. especially the publications of the Yiddish Scientific Institute (YIVO).

4. See references to the Indian national culture society in Chapters Two and Three.

5. See, e.g., George Antonius, *The Arab Awakening* (Philadelphia: Lippincott, 1939); Bertram Thomas, *The Arabs* (Garden City, N. Y.: Doubleday, 1937); T. E. Lawrence, *Seven Pillars of Wisdom* (Garden City, N. Y.: Doubleday, 1938); Antoine Zischka, *Die Auferstehung Arabiens* (Leipzig, 1935); Michel Laisay, *Du Panarabisme à la Ligue Arabe* (Paris, 1948); Murray Wittner, *The Unification of Arabian National Culture* (manuscript).

regulate social actions follow the principles contained in the sacred books: ethics was, and is, religious ethics in Brahmanism, Buddhism, Judaism, Zoroastrianism, Christianity, Islam. Indeed, the ethical system of the Roman Catholic Church has often been termed "moral theology." The same is true of certain legal codes, e.g., the Laws of Manu and most of the legislation in Mohammedan states. Mythology has strongly influenced poetry also: e.g., the two great Hindu epics, *Māhābhārata* and *Ramayana*. The music included in religious cultus is differentiated from folk music and eventually professionalized. Architecture, sculpture, and painting, developed in building and decorating temples under the patronage or control of priests, acquire a sacred significance, and consequently have to conform with the requirements of mythology and collective cultus. Even the production and use of material values with no sacred meaning—agriculture, horticulture, animal husbandry, craftsmanship—is often expected to be preceded or followed by religious performances. Religious control of material culture was most fully developed in India, where specialized technical actions could be exclusively performed by hereditary members of certain castes, and the entire differentiation of castes was subjected to strict religious sanctions.

National cultures are harder to define and circumscribe, for they lack the permanent, authoritative foundation which sacred books provide. We must rely here on modern historians of national cultures—French, Italian, English, Spanish, German, Polish, Russian—and these historians differ somewhat as to what cultural products and patterns of action are components of a particular culture. We find that most of them treat as the basic component of a national culture a common literary language, used mainly in secular literature, which eventually becomes standardized in dictionaries and grammars. All kinds of works originally written in this language are viewed by historians as parts of the national literature. Such a literature includes works of legend and fiction, recognized as such, legal and philosophic theories, works classified under the categories of "humanities" and "social sciences": political science, economics, history, folklore and ethnology, theory of art, musicology; finally, works concerning natural sciences, theoretic and applied.

A well-known problem arises when the same literary language is used by writers who by other standards are considered participants in different nationalities—e.g., the English literary language by Englishmen, Irishmen, and Americans; Spanish by Spaniards, Mexicans, Chileans, Peruvians, and Argentineans. Here the nationality or political citizenship of the author is used as criterion in deciding to which national culture his works belong.

Products of plastic arts and musical compositions are also included in the national culture, if the artists or composers are considered by historians as belonging or having belonged to the collectivity which shares this culture. For instance, historians of art classify together all the creative works of artists of various schools in various states and cities of Italy which have been produced since the beginning of the Renaissance, as constituting "Italian art," because the artists are considered "Italians." The same conception is applied to music. Historians designate by the terms "Italian music," "German music," "French music," "Russian music," all the musical works created by "Italians," "Germans," "Frenchmen," "Russians."

As we shall see later, many historians include within their national cultures various components of local and regional folk cultures which existed before national language and literature appeared. They do so under the assumption that, since national cultures partly evolved from these folk cultures, and the peoples who maintained the former were ancestors of those who developed the latter, they already belonged to the same nationality—were Italians, Spaniards, Frenchmen, and Germans, though still unaware of it.

While national cultures are continually growing, we notice

14

in recent times attempts to develop what may be called a *world civilization* or *world culture*. Some religious thinkers hope to integrate various religious cultures into a universal religion. Certain communist leaders expect to superimpose a new universal culture—originally called "proletarian"—upon all national cultures. Quite a few leaders promoting cultural cooperation between nationalities are trying to initiate the creative evolution of new ideational systems and patterns of action which would eventually be accepted by all mankind, irrespective of national and religious differences. We must postpone the discussion of these trends.

Social organization of a national culture society

It is not our task as sociologists to study the content of national cultures in their totality. Philosophers of history tried to do this in the eighteenth and nineteenth centuries. Many of them were fully aware that what is called "secular" culture or civilization develops much later than religious culture. But in consequence of the progress of historical methods and discoveries during the nineteenth century, a thorough, systematic investigation of even one modern nationality proves to be a tremendous undertaking. Adequate knowledge of English, French, or German aesthetic literature—epics, dramas, lyrics, novels—or of philosophic literature, or of the plastic arts requires years of study. Furthermore, national cultures as totalities differ so much from each other that attempts to draw comparative generalizations about them are of doubtful validity.

The problem with which we are concerned here is strictly sociological. It is well known that a common national culture, just as a common religious culture, is a basis for social solidarity, uniting the people who share it, and may be an important source of conflict between them and peoples who have different national cultures. This solidarity is not merely a matter of subjective mass psychology, of common feelings and volitions, for it is objectively manifested in effective collective activities. And, as we have pointed out, no complex culture can exist without the continuous active cooperation of the individuals and groups who maintain its existence. This means that the people who share a national culture must, in some measure at least, be socially organized.

The study of this type of social organization falls within the domain of sociology, but has been rather neglected. Sociology was from the beginning conceived as a science of organized human collectivities, called "societies." The concept of society, however, was defined in a way which limited its application exclusively to *territorially circumscribed* collectivities. A society was conceived as including all the people inhabiting for generations a definite territory, with an integrated social structure which separates it from all other territorial societies and a common and distinctive culture embodied in a system of institutions. This conception, initiated by Comte, was fully developed by Spencer and continues to dominate sociological thought. A distinction is often made between primitive, lower, nonliterate, or tribal societies and higher or civilized societies, with intermediary types between them. The universal characteristic of higher societies is a well-organized *political* system.

Such a conception of society is obviously too narrow. In the first place, it ignores the fact that in the modern world parts of the population of many states can share the same religious culture; consequently, much of their social life is controlled and integrated not by the state, but by the Church, which has a distinct social organization of its own, often cutting across political boundaries. Nor is the collectivity which shares a modern national culture necessarily coextensive with any state. For instance, throughout the nineteenth century and up to World War I, the people who shared Polish national culture were subdivided into demographic sections included within the territories of three states, each of which controlled politically

16

its Polish subjects. Between World Wars I and II, more than ten million people who shared German culture (not counting the Austrians or the Swiss) lived outside of the German Reich, in areas located within various states of Europe and America. The territory of Great Britain includes peoples of three different national cultures: the English, Scottish, and Welsh—not to mention the Irish. But people of English culture live in politically autonomous dominions, territorially located in North America, Australia, New Zealand, and Africa. Within the territory of the United States of America there are millions of inhabitants, most of them citizens, who share with people living outside of the United States some one of at least forty-five different national cultures. Obviously, whatever common social organization enables these peoples to preserve their national cultures is not a part of any political organization.

The sociological concept of society must be, therefore, either dropped or redefined so as to include different collectivities with partly overlapping membership. We believe that it can be so redefined, because a comparative analysis of the social organization of these collectivities shows certain important similarities underlying their differences. Let us compare briefly the social organization of a preliterate tribe, a modern state, and a large Church which extends into the territories of several states.

Each of these collectivities includes a number of people belonging to several successive generations. Participation in each is limited by definite standards which permanently distinguish its members from nonmembers, or outsiders. As we mentioned before, membership in a tribe—e.g., the Navaho Indians or the Masai—is usually limited to those who are supposed to be descendants of common ancestors. Though a tribe usually inhabits a certain territory, it can remain united and distinct from other tribes even if it migrates to another territory. A modern state (e.g., Great Britain or the United States or Russia) includes all the people who inhabit a certain circumscribed

17

territory and are subjected to the control of the same government, even though they are not of common descent. The Roman
Catholic Church includes all those who share the same religious beliefs and practices, even though they are territorially
scattered over the world and have no common origin.

Now, in every one of these collectivities, most of the actions
of participants conform with definite cultural standards and
norms and involve some degree of social cooperation. Every
individual in the course of his life performs specific social roles
which include certain duties toward several others and certain
rights which those others grant to him. Furthermore, in every
relatively large collectivity, we find a number of social groups
each of which is composed of individuals who act collectively
for certain common purposes. These are the basic social systems
which every human collectivity contains.

However, in the three types of collectivities mentioned
above there is a considerable degree of functional integration
of specific social roles and of specific social groups or associations. The tribe, the state, the Church in its totality is considered by many, if not by all, of its participants as very important and valuable, and some social roles as well as some
social groups are supposed to function permanently on its behalf; the actions which these individuals and groups regularly
perform are considered essential for the continued existence of
the collectivity as a whole. These functions differ greatly; and
the more different they are, the more complex the social organization of the collectivity.

Thus, in a nonliterate tribe all adult participants perform
definite roles, including various technical actions by which each
of them helps satisfy certain needs of some others and satisfies
his own needs with the aid of some others. Most adults also
protect and educate their young descendants. They and their
descendants belong to definite social groups—families, small or
large, cooperative groups, each of which acts on behalf of its
members. However, some men (sometimes even women), pre-

18

sumably endowed with superior mystical power, perform magical and religious functions on which not merely the welfare of particular individuals, but the welfare and security of the whole tribe, is supposed to depend. Also, final preparation of the young for full membership in the tribe is carried on not individually by their older relatives, but collectively in initiation ceremonies under the guidance of competent leaders, because otherwise the tribe as an integrated community could not last. In many tribes, men function on certain occasions as warriors in defense or aggression against an enemy tribe; this function is obviously considered important for the tribe as a whole. A tribe usually has a chief (who may or may not be also a leader of warriors) whose main function is to maintain order among its members and thus to preserve the unity of the tribe; the chief may have a circle of assistants and advisers.

We are familiar with the main functions, widely diversified and well integrated, which some individuals and groups perform on behalf of the collectivity of people who compose a modern state. They are sometimes called "public functions," as distinct from the vast multiplicity of "private functions" performed by individuals acting on behalf of other individuals and by those numerous and various groups which are not institutional components of that complex system which is termed "government." Survey, for instance, the public functions of the United States of America as a Federal state, with its forty-eight state divisions and territorial subdivisions within each state. Consider the various executive roles, with the President at the top, heads of executive departments of the Federal government, heads of special divisions within each department, governors of states and their auxiliary functionaries. Take the legislative roles of delegates of states to the Federal legislature and delegates of territorial divisions within each state to the legislative body of the state. Take the various juridical roles, from the judges of the United States Supreme Court down to local justices of the peace. Take the numerous and diverse

19

governmental groups and subgroups functioning on behalf of the United States and of each particular state: the United States Congress and state legislatures; civil departments with widely differentiated functions, and their territorial subdivisions; military groups and subgroups with special branches; technical groups taking care of governmental properties; etc.

Not quite so complex, but at least as well-integrated functionally, are the public social roles and the social groups within the Roman Catholic Church. There is, first, the large class of priestly roles, with a hierarchy graded from the Pope through cardinals, archbishops, bishops, down to ordinary priests. Within this general class we find considerable functional differentiation of roles. The majority of priests function as administrators, but others are legislators, jurists, diplomats, missionaries, theologians, scholars, scientists. Of the numerous and diverse social groups functioning on behalf of the Church we may mention: monastic orders, educational groups—seminaries, universities, secondary and primary schools—groups of librarians and of musicians, associations of priests and laymen trying to spread and realize certain political or economic ideals or to counteract the spread and realization of ideals which conflict with the doctrines of the Church.

If the term "society" is applicable to such different collectivities as a preliterate tribe and the United States, because each has a rather integrated, separate, and independent social organization of its own, it can certainly be applied also to the collectivity called the Roman Catholic Church. And in a comparative investigation of collectivities which possess distinctive national cultures, we find that most of these collectivities in the course of history have already developed or are developing a combination of specific social roles and social groups which function on behalf of the collectivity as a whole. Although their organization is less formal than that of a state and less stable than that of a Church, it is sufficiently integrated to call them "societies."

Thus, we may distinguish at least four types of society. First, the old, preliterate *tribal society*. However important from the point of view of students of culture, it has very little influence in the modern world and is gradually disappearing. We shall leave it out of this survey. Second, the *political society*, or *state*, which has a common legal system and an organized, independent government controlling all the people who inhabit a definite territory. Third, the *ecclesiastical society*, which has a common and distinct literary, religious culture and an independent, organized church. Fourth, the *national culture society*, which has a common and distinct secular, literary culture and an independent organization functioning for the preservation, growth, and expansion of this culture. We would prefer a simpler term to denote this fourth type, but none can be devised in English, and we have tried in vain to coin a new, compound Greek term. In this outline, we shall occasionally use the popular term "nationality" as a substitute for the more complex term "national culture society" as defined above.

Perhaps we should already recognize a fifth type of society—a *world society*. This ideal, long cherished by thinkers and leaders, has, I believe, begun to be realized.[6]

In the light of this comparative analysis, we shall define the term "nationalism" as the active solidarity of a national culture society.

6. We cannot discuss here in detail the difference between a society and a social group. For our present task, it will be enough to state that social groups (with the exception of so-called primary groups, like families, clans, neighborhoods, village-communities, which could not be called societies in any case) are differentiated by their specialized functions, i.e., by the specific purposes which they collectively pursue. These explain, for instance, the obvious differences between a factory, a bank, a scientific or artistic association, a labor union, an association of manufacturers, a political party, a country club, a school, a consumers' cooperative, a religious sect. Whereas a society, as we have noticed, contains a number of specialized social groups, which together contribute to its continued existence. This distinction, however, cannot be applied to a modern city. The total population of London, Paris, New York, or San Francisco (unlike that of ancient Sparta or early Rome) is not a separate and united whole. As a territorial collectivity with a municipal government, it is an integral part of a larger political society; its inhabitants are divided between several ecclesiastical societies, each extending far beyond its territorial limits; it contains several national collectivities, each sharing a distinct literary culture with millions of people living in other urban and rural areas, sometimes even on another continent.

21

two

the origin of

national culture societies

Who initiates the formation of a national culture society?

When we survey the history of nationalism during the last two hundred years, we notice that some nationalities began to manifest strong active solidarity much earlier than others. Thus, in Europe at the beginning of the nineteenth century common national culture was already a powerful bond uniting Frenchmen, Englishmen, Irishmen, Danes, Swedes, Poles, Czechs, Russians, Greeks, Hungarians; although some political and economic conflicts occurred within each nationality, they were less influential and lasting than conflicts between nationalities. Italian and German cultural solidarity, though already strong, did not overcome political divisions and conflicts until after the middle of the century. The cultural solidarity of Finns, Estonians, Letts, Lithuanians, Ukrainians, Slovaks was fully manifested only in the twentieth century.

Outside of Europe no such solidarity existed a century and a half ago. The American colonies broke away from England while they still shared English culture. An original American culture soon began to develop, but ninety years ago it was not yet sufficiently strong as a social bond to prevent a civil war; however, during the last seventy-five years, its unifying influence has been steadily growing. In Spanish America, notwithstanding a common historical background of Spanish culture, separate sovereign states were formed; interstate wars and civil wars have been going on for more than a century, and only recently did new original national cultures begin to grow in some of them. In Asia, Chinese culture, which for centuries united a small group of intellectuals, is not yet sufficiently influential to unite the masses of Chinese people. Japanese unity proved strong, indeed, during the last fifty years, but we must remember that the people who share Japanese national culture have also some age-old common religious beliefs, and nearly all belong to a well-integrated political society. In India, the

23

1. For a general survey of the early stages of growing national solidarity in Asia, see Hans Kohn, *Geschichte der Nationalen bewegung im Orient* (Berlin, 1928). Similar growth has started in several regions of Africa. According to J. Obrebski, "The great revolution of our times consists . . . in the formation of new national cultures and national culture groups." "The Sociology of Rising Nations," *International Social Science Bulletin*, No. 2, 1951, III, 238.

2. A number of my students supplemented my work by their own historical surveys of the evolution of particular nationalities, using the conceptual framework formulated in this and the next chapter.

The following nationalities were surveyed: American, during the colonial era, by Theodore Fish; Armenian, by Gregory N. Cross; Brazilian, by Joyce Hooper; Burmese, by Sheldon Davidson; Colombian, by Wilma Ernst; Indian, since independence, by Robert W. Fox; Irish, by V. Sutcher; Jewish, by Joyce Kaplan; Korean, by Edmund L. Szablowski; Lithuanian, by A. J. Krukas; Mexican, by Shirley Horwitz and by Lois Sprout; Nigerian, by Joyce Wiener; Peruvian, by Earl Rubeking; Rumanian, by Philip Ackerman; Uruguayan, by Wilma Ernst; Welsh, by Jane Mueller.

religious solidarity and separatism of Moslems and Hindus are more powerful than the ideal of a common Indian cultural nationality promulgated by nationalistic leaders. Of Islamic peoples, only the Turks already form a separate, united nationality; a distinctly Arabian national unity has only recently begun to develop.[1]

This brief survey indicates that, in order to compare national culture societies and reach sociological generalizations about them, we cannot simply study them as they exist right now or as they once did exist at any particular static cross section of universal history. We must investigate them in the course of their gradual development from the time of their origin. A comparative analysis of this development shows that, however much the cultures differ, the processes of their social formation, growth, and integration manifest a striking similarity.[2]

In every instance hitherto investigated, the formation of a national culture society starts with a relatively small social nucleus whose influence slowly spreads until it eventually reaches millions of people. This nucleus is not constituted by any authoritative organized group, be it the government of a state, or the clerical hierarchy of a church, or an association of members of an economically dominant class. It originates with independent *individual leaders* in various realms of cultural activity, who gradually create a national culture in which a plurality of traditional regional cultures becomes partly synthesized. We call them leaders because and insofar as they attract circles of voluntary followers. They frequently gain also the support of socially powerful sponsors or patrons—princes, magnates, church dignitaries, men of wealth, statesmen, military commanders, heads of political parties.

As the national culture grows, these leaders, their followers, and sponsors who participate in its growth form an increasingly coherent intellectual community activated by the ideal of a culturally united and socially solidary national society, which should include all the people whose folk cultures are presumed to be essentially alike and who are supposed to share the same historical background. The realization of this ideal is expected to overcome the cultural isolation of local and regional communities, political divisions, religious differences, class conflicts. We shall see later by what methods this ideal becomes realized.

Throughout this process new social groups become organized and existing groups modified, either to promote further development and perpetuation of the national culture or to integrate, expand, and defend the evolving society.

Let us survey, first, the various social roles of those intellectual leaders who contribute to the creative growth of a national culture.

The social roles of men of letters

We use the term "men of letters" to denote writers of aesthetic works. It is they who developed new literary languages from traditional regional dialects and produced distinctive nationalistic literatures. They did this by recording and synthesizing in writing the unwritten products of popular poetry, myth, legend, and story; by translating into the vernacular or imitating the aesthetic products of older literatures; and especially by their own original creations. These writers initiated national cultures in Western and Central Europe at the time when the only fully developed literary culture in these areas (apart from Hebrew culture, shared by scattered Jewish communities) was that of the Roman Catholic Church, which throughout its extent used Latin as a common language.

Of course, men of letters were not the only ones who contributed to the formation of new literary languages. Some early legal documents were written in the vernacular. Priests translated prayers and wrote sermons in a popular language which could be understood by inhabitants of a large region. Eventually, when the Reformation began, important contributions to the standardization, unification, and spread of national languages were made by Protestant leaders who translated the Bible into the vernacular in order to make it accessible to lay believers. Thus, John Huss and his successors translated it into Czech, Wycliffe into English, Luther into German. Catholics followed their example later, at a time when the national languages were already at least partly developed.

Now, why was the development of national cultures mainly due to writers of aesthetic literature? To answer this question adequately, we would have to explain the universal appeal, in traditional as well as in literary cultures, of epics, legends, fiction, lyric poetry, drama; and this is, of course, far beyond our present task. The significant point about the social roles of secular men of letters as initiators and builders of national culture is that, unlike religious writers and legislators, they had considerable freedom of innovation. Their agglomerated original contributions enriched the language in which they wrote, besides giving new aesthetic form and new content to the total literature which they were creating. At the same time, however, some linguistic standards and norms had to be accepted by all writers who used the same language; otherwise, this language would have no cultural unity or continuity. Consequently, after the Renaissance, dictionaries and grammars of modern national languages began to be composed on the model of dictionaries and grammars of ancient Greek and Latin.

The creative growth of national languages and literatures, however, was rather slow, especially when writers used different regional dialects as main foundations for a new literary language. This is well exemplified in France. French literature began in the eleventh century with the *Chansons de Geste,* epic stories about the achievements of military heroes, and later with lyric poetry. In the thirteenth century, two different literary languages were evolving in France: one based on southern dialects, popularly included under the name "langue d'oc"; the other on northern dialects, under the name "langue d'oil."

Which of the competing regional dialects eventually triumphed and became accepted as the common national literary language depended, first, upon the number, as well as upon the wealth of form and of content, of the literary works created by the authors who used it; second, upon the support of influential sponsors who helped spread it over several regions. Thus, the literature of southern France ceased to grow after the Albigensian war, whereas the literature of northern France continued to grow, slowly at first, more and more rapidly during the sixteenth and seventeenth centuries, when its spread was sponsored by the kings of France.

The language originally based on the Tuscan dialect became universally recognized and accepted as the supreme common Italian language at the beginning of the fourteenth century, due to the many creative contributions written in that language, culminating in the works of Dante and Petrarch. The Norman conquest impeded the development of Old English, based on Anglo-Saxon dialects, and only in the fifteenth century did Modern English begin to grow creatively through new contributions. From about 1150 on, the German literary language, based on so-called High German (*hoch deutsch*), was sponsored by several rulers and autonomous cities, although only about 1500 did it gain general recognition as the national language, as shown by the fact that Luther used it for his translation of the Bible.[3] No such difficulty, however, in overcoming dialectical differences was found in Poland. Up to the end of the fifteenth century, Latin was the language used by nearly all Polish writers. When in the sixteenth century Polish national literature began to develop, most of the writers were nobles, and by that time the spoken language of the nobility was already quite uniform; only the regional dialects used by peasants continued to differ widely.

The evolution of new national languages and literatures

3. A. F. C. Vilmar, *Geschichte der Deutschen National-Literatur* (Marburg-Leipzig, 1894).

27

4. Some Ukrainian historians trace its beginning to the twelfth century, e.g., Mitropolit Ilarion, *History of Ukrainian Literary Language*, in Ukrainian (Winnipeg, 1950). However, at that time, in consequence of many migrations, the specific regional dialects were not yet separated and stabilized. What later became a distinct and common Ukrainian literature was growing slowly, though the influence of Old Slavonic remained strong until the nineteenth century. For its full development in modern times, see, e.g., D. Doroshenko, *History of the Ukraine* (Edmonton, 1940); Michael Hrushevsky, *A History of Ukraine* (New Haven: Yale University Press, 1941).

5. See Alexander Brückner, *A Literary History of Russia*, trans. by H. Havelock (New York: Scribner, 1908). An excellent outline of the beginnings and subsequent growth of literature in Russia.

was much slower in Eastern Europe. Greek became the religious literary language of the Greek Orthodox Church; but, unlike Latin, it remained at the same time a spoken language, used by several million people. There was no linguistic distinction between religious and secular language, and contributions to Greek literature continued to be made as long as the Byzantine Empire lasted. But after the Ottoman conquest, Greek secular literature practically disappeared; only in the nineteenth century did a new literature, written in modern Greek, begin to develop.

In order to promote the conversion of Slavs in the Danube region, Cyril and Methodius in the ninth century translated the Bible into a new written language which they introduced. It was based upon the Slavic dialects of this region, with an alphabet borrowed from Greek, but somewhat modified to fit the local dialects. This language, later called "Old Slavonic," was also used to spread Christianity among the Eastern Slavs north of the Balkans and remained for nearly a thousand years an almost changeless sacred literary language of all the Slavic peoples who did not adopt the Latin language as used by the Roman Catholic Church. In the course of time, secular works appeared, combining in various degrees this Old Slavonic with regional dialects; and eventually several national languages with distinctive literatures evolved, but with one exception this evolution was interrupted or slowed down by extraneous influences. Thus, the Ottoman invasion of the Balkans stopped the incipient development of the Serbian and the Bulgarian literatures, which did not start again until the nineteenth century. The growth of the Ukrainian national literature was until recent times impeded by the influence of Polish culture in the west and repressed in the east by the Tsarist regime.[4] On the other hand, Russian (or "Great Russian") literature, although it began to develop only in the eighteenth century, has been growing rapidly and continuously.[5]

The problem of developing a secular literary language to be used by all the people belonging to the same nationality has not yet been solved by Jewish or by Hindu leaders. During the development of Jewish national culture (as distinct from Hebrew religious culture), Yiddish literature has grown rapidly. But Zionist leaders refuse to accept Yiddish as the common literary language; they promote instead the revival of Hebrew not only as sacred, but also as secular, language. In India, the most widely spread literary language is Hindustani, but less than a third of the people of India understand it; moreover, it has two different divisions, one used by Moslems, the other by Hindus. Similarly, a dual trend is found in Ireland: Should Gaelic be fully revived or English used in Irish literature? [6] Of course, it may be said that a common language is not indispensable for social unity, as the example of Switzerland shows. But the Swiss form a political society, including three nationalities, not a national culture society. [7]

The example of older and more developed national culture societies has made leaders striving for the cultural independence and social unification of their own nationality fully aware of the importance of creating an original national literature. For instance, the growth of Norwegian literature has been recognized as the most important step in liberating the Norwegian people from the century-old cultural and social domination of the Danish national society. [8] After gaining political independence from Spain and Portugal, the striving of Latin American political societies for cultural independence was manifested sooner or later in efforts to develop original literatures of their own. [9] In British Canada, the creative growth of an original Canadian literature is considered the most important step toward the development of a separate Canadian nationality, united by a distinctive, independent culture of its own.

6. Douglas Hyde, *A Literary History of Ireland* (London, 1901); Ernst A. Boyod, *Ireland's Literary Renaissance* (New York: Day, 1916); Aodh de Blácam, *Gaelic Literature Surveyed* (Dublin, 1929); Emma Jane Williams, "The Celtic Renaissance" (manuscript). Systematic attempts to revive Gaelic continue to this day, not only in Ireland but among Irish immigrants abroad. For instance, in 1949, there were five Gaelic societies in New York (Austin Hershberger, manuscript).

7. Four, if we include Romansh, which is more a folk dialect than a literary language.

8. Cf. Agnes M. Wergeland, *Leaders in Norway* (Menasha, Wis.: Banta, 1916); Einar I. Hangen, *The Origin and Early History of the New Norse Movement in Norway* (Menasha, Wis.: Modern Language Association, 1933); A. Sommerfelt, *The Written and Spoken Word in Norway* (Oxford, 1942).

9. Cf., e.g., R. Craig, *The Modernistic Trend in Spanish-American Poetry* (Berkeley: University of California Press, 1934); Isaac J. Barrera, *Literatura Hispano-americana* (Quito, 1934); Alfred L. Coester, *The*

The social roles of historians and ethnographers

While a common written language and literature is a necessary condition of overcoming the separatism of local and regional collectivities with different folk cultures, it is obviously not sufficient to integrate socially such collectivities. The very idea that they should be united is founded upon the doctrine that, however much their folk cultures may differ, they are essentially similar as compared with those of other collectivities and that this similarity is essentially due to a common historical background. This doctrine is a joint product of ethnographers who study folk cultures and of historians who trace back the origin of these cultures and of the peoples who maintain them. Ethnography and history are both very old and from the beginning they have been interconnected.

Members of a tribe or a folk community are aware that their cultural products, customs, and mores differ from those of other tribes or communities with which they have been in contact and are in some measure acquainted. And, whenever there is considerable social mobility, especially mass migrations, tribes come into contact with other tribes, hitherto unknown, whose cultures differ more from theirs than the cultures of their neighbors do. They become increasingly conscious of the fundamental similarities underlying what in the light of these new contacts appears to be only minor differences. Such primitive ethnographic knowledge, however superficial and prejudiced, has been the original source from which comparative studies of culture have evolved.

As to primitive history, we know that all tribes and folk communities are conscious of a common past. Older members can name their predecessors for several generations back, and any important event affecting the life of the collectivity becomes part of the traditional knowledge transmitted from generation to generation. Of course, the more distant the past, the less reliable the oral history, until eventually it becomes mere legend.

Literary History of Spanish America (New York: Macmillan, 1941); Julio A. Leguizamón, *Historia de la Literatura Hispano-Americana*, 2 vols. (Buenos Aires, 1945); Isaac Goldberg, *Brazilian Literature* (New York: Knopf, 1922); José Bezerra de Freitas, *História da Literatura Brasileira* (Pôrto Alegre, 1939); Erico Verissimo, *Brazilian Literature, an Outline* (New York: Macmillan, 1945).

It is curious that, while the literary works written in Portuguese by authors living in Brazil are treated as a separate "Brazilian literature," all the literary works written in Spanish by authors living in Central and South America are included under the general term "Spanish-American literature," instead of being particularized as "Mexican literature," "Peruvian literature," "Argentinean literature," etc. Can this be the manifestation of an incipient tendency to develop cultural solidarity among all the peoples in the Americas who share the Spanish literary language, over and above the cultural nationalism growing in the particular countries?

And in most collectivities with traditional cultures, we find myths and legends which explain the origin of the most permanent, important, and valuable components of their culture as creations of certain ancestors who, if not divine beings, were at least superhuman heroes. Such explanations have a dual significance; they strengthen the belief of members of the collectivity in the supreme validity of their culture and in their own superiority as heirs of such great ancestors.

When written history began, the historians were mostly priests, and they originally assumed a common descent of the people who shared the same religion, as they did in the Old Testament. Frequently, however, religious history was closely connected with the political history of the kingdom ruled by a sacred king. The separation of the two was partly achieved by Chinese historians, fully by Greek and Roman historians, who specialized almost entirely in political history. But the old connection between history and ethnography remained as exemplified by Herodotus' description of Persian, Egyptian, and other Eastern peoples. And nearly all Greek historians, even those who limited their histories to particular city-states or wars, considered Hellenes as culturally and hereditarily superior to Barbarians. During the Middle Ages, priests again assumed the function of historians, but political history remained distinct from the history of the Church, though strongly influenced by religious ideology. This is well exemplified by the two works of Grégoire de Tours, written in the sixth century: ten books on the *History of the Franks* and six books on the *Miracles* performed by Frankish saints.

When secular history began to be written by secular authors, it was primarily political, especially when historians functioned under the patronage of rulers, and much of it remains political to this day, though for different reasons, such as the facility of obtaining political and legal documents and of reconstructing from them political organizations. Gradually, however, cultural similarities and differences not coextensive with political divisions began to be taken into consideration by historians. Ethnographic knowledge of these similarities and differences was at first rather superficial, derived mostly from the observations of travelers (including merchants) and from contacts of natives with foreign travelers, immigrants, and invaders; only from the second half of the eighteenth century on did ethnographic studies of folk cultures begin to provide factual foundation for including some of these cultures in the same nationality and excluding others. For instance, Herder, who was both an ethnographer and a philosopher of history, used his studies of German folk culture as a basis for his conception of the historical unity and continuity of the German people. But even as early as the end of the fifteenth century, many intellectuals had already formed definite cultural stereotypes of "Italians," "Spaniards," "Frenchmen," "Englishmen," "Germans," etc., although the stereotypes naturally differed, according to the nationality to which the intellectuals themselves belonged. And this was the time when historians started to write histories of nationalities.

Italian historians, for example, who at first wrote exclusively histories of particular city-states, gradually began to write historical works dealing with Italy as a whole.[10] This was not merely because the Italian peninsula formed a definite territorial unit, but chiefly because of the common culture of Italian people, mainly derived from the dominant Latin culture of the Roman Empire. Later, some French historians included in the history of France, besides the state ruled by the kings of France, other areas which were not parts of this state, but were inhabited by people who, whatever their regional differences, were presumably like the Frenchmen within the kingdom, because they had the common historical background of Romanized Gaul. This trend culminated in the early nineteenth century, and is well exemplified by the work of Théophile Lavallée on the history of the French since the time of the Gauls.[11]

10. Francesco Guicciardini, *La Historia di Italia* (Florence, 1561), was the first historical work of this type, limited to the preceding years and not very optimistic.

11. Théophile Lavallée, *Histoire des Français depuis le temps des Gaulois jusqu'en 1830*, 1st ed. (Paris, 1838).

32

German historians dealing with the history of the medieval empire conceived it from the very first as an empire "der deutschen Nation," under the obvious assumption that it was composed of people of common German descent and culture. Later, they began to write histories of the "German people" as a whole, culturally united long before the empire was formed. Thus, Sporschil wrote a work on the history of the Germans from the oldest times up to his day, beginning with the struggle against Rome in the second century B.C. After the Nazis came to power, Pastenaci published a book in German entitled *The Four-Thousand-Year-Old Kingdom of the Germans.*[12]

Polish historians to this very day have been primarily concerned with the history of all the peoples who have shared the common Polish culture, presumably rooted in a prehistoric past, notwithstanding their political division in the thirteenth century and the nonexistence of an independent Polish state from 1795 to 1918. Modern Russian history started in the eighteenth century as a history of the multiple nationalities in the Tsarist Empire,[13] but eventually Russia was conceived as culturally Russian, including all the peoples (mostly Slavs) who presumably already shared or were expected to share the culture of the dominant Great Russian nationality.[14]

Both historians and ethnographers usually tend to emphasize the distinctive character of their own nationality, and many of them are inclined to exalt it as superior to others, at least in some respects, just as religious thinkers, political thinkers, even tribal thinkers exalt their own societies.[15] This has been called by some sociologists "national megalomania." We shall mention here a few examples.

The superiority of Chinese people was for centuries taken for granted by Chinese historians; nor was this belief undermined by the Manchu conquest, since the conquerors accepted Chinese culture. In modern Europe, Italian scholars were probably the first to exalt their history, culture, and nationality,

12. Johann Sporschil, *Geschichte der Deutschen von den ältesten Zeiten,* 5 vols. (Regensburg, 1859-60); Kurt Pastenaci, *Das viertausendjährige Reich der Deutschen* (Berlin, 1940).

13. Some minor outlines, e.g., Tatishchev. The first comprehensive history of the Russian state, exalting autocracy, was written by N. Karamzin, 12 vols. (1818-26).

14. As early as 1831, the poet Pushkin wrote that all the "Slavonic streams" were destined to merge in the "Russian Sea." By the end of the nineteenth century all Russian textbooks emphasized the predominantly "Russian" character of most of the inhabitants of the empire.

15. The significance of history in the development of modern nationalism was noticed some time ago. See, e.g., R. W. Seton-Watson, *The Historian as a Political Force in Central Europe* (London, 1922).

and many continue to do so still. This has provided comfort and confidence for all the people who were conscious of being Italians, especially at times of crisis, during periods of inner conflict and of foreign domination. This exaltation had three foundations. First, Italians were the heirs of Roman greatness. Dante initiated this conception, but it was fully developed only recently by Mussolini and his followers. Second, the creative growth of Italian national culture began relatively early in Italy and was for a long time a model which other nationalities imitated. Third, Rome was, and is, the world center of Catholicism, and Rome is Italian.

Quite a few French historians have exalted the total history of the French nationality. For instance. Lavallée in his preface to the *Histoire des Français* states: "I have considered France as exerting at all epochs the moral leadership of Europe, as having providentially the mission of progress, as always placed at the head of other nations so as to trace for them the road for the future; thus, the history of our country has been for me the history of humanity in the West." At about the same time, Hegel as philosopher of history was developing his theory that German civilization (a synthesis of two antithetic civilizations, oriental and Greco-Roman) was the supreme "objective" manifestation of the "Absolute Spirit." A century later, A. Willy and W. von Scholz published a work *Die grossen Deutschen,* five volumes of idealized biographies, proving the age-old supremacy of the Germans in every realm of culture.[16]

In Russia, about the middle of the nineteenth century, while so-called "Westerners" deplored the lag of Russian culture and urged it to follow the West, "Slavophiles" exalted the greatness of the Russian people as supreme representatives of the old Slavonic culture which was morally and spiritually superior to every other.[17] Later, as original Russian culture, especially literature, music, and art, grew, the "West" lost its influence. After the October Revolution, Bolshevik historians at first disparaged the Russian national culture developed during the

16. A. Willy and W. von Scholz, *Die grossen Deutschen* (Berlin, 1935-37). For a survey of such trends in German historiography, see Antoine Guilland, *Modern Germany and Her Historians* (New York: McBride, 1915).

17. Khomyakóv, Kiréevsky, and Aksakov. Perhaps the most enthusiastic proclaimer of the greatness of the Russian "national spirit" was Dostoyevsky. Cf. Hans Kohn, *Prophets and Peoples* (New York: Macmillan, 1946), Chap. V.

Tsarist regime on the ground that it was "bourgeois"; but they soon revived its positive valuation, and naturally extolled the new cultural developments under the Communist regime. By now Russian culture is supposed to be far in advance of any other.

The emergence of nationalism in India was from the very first influenced by the intellectual leaders, who compared the history of Hindu civilization with the history of modern Western civilizations and exalted the former as representing the highest spiritual values in contrast to the latter, which are essentially materialistic.

The social roles of national ideologists

While historians are studying the past, we find in every nationality intellectual leaders who are thinking about its future and promulgating ideals which they expect to be realized by their society. We call them *ideologists*. Poets and even historians sometimes function as ideologists, but the most influential of them are usually philosophers of values. Not all ideologists, however, are nationalistic; some are concerned with the future of humanity, and the ideals which they formulate are meant to be realized by all mankind.

The influence of ideologists upon the development of national culture societies depends upon the acceptance of their ideals, not merely by other thinkers, but by active followers and sponsors who work for the realization of their ideals and—most important—upon the formation of social groups organized for this purpose.

We find four main ideals promulgated by nationalistic thinkers:

1. The ideal of national unification
2. The ideal of national progress
3. The ideal of a national mission
4. The ideal of national independence

1. The ideal of national unification. When a national culture begins to grow and certain ethnographers and historians develop the conception of a culturally distinct nationality with a common past, the people who are supposed to belong to this nationality are seldom united solidarily; various divisions and conflicts among them make active solidarity difficult, sometimes even impossible, to attain. Then intellectual leaders, aware of this lack of solidarity, promulgate ideals which, if realized, would overcome those divisions and conflicts and result in a united society with a common culture as lasting bond.

Political divisions are the most obvious obstacles to national unity. The division of Italy into a number of separate city-states struggling for power and competing for wealth stimulated Italian thinkers, beginning with Machiavelli, to promulgate the ideal of political unification. However, the first attempts to realize this ideal were impeded by foreign influences. Italy in the sixteenth century became the battleground of foreign powers, and various parts of Italy were for longer or shorter periods subjected to foreign domination. Consequently, the ideal of political unification became connected with the ideal of national independence. But it took three centuries for these ideals to be realized.

When the unity of the feudal German Empire, never very strong, broke down, and political conflicts between separate states grew in violence (especially during the Thirty Years' War), political unification of the German people gradually became the main ideal of German nationalistic thinkers.[18] From the middle of the eighteenth century on and more particularly under the impact of the Napoleonic invasion, this ideal gained adherents.[19] It was realized partially in 1871 and fully under the Nazi regime, but then for only a few years.

Beginning in the second half of the nineteenth century, Hindu leaders, like the earlier Italian leaders, promulgated both the ideal of national independence and the ideal of political unification. But the case of India differs from that

18. Definitely by Herder, but also by Lessing, Wieland, and others.

19. Cf. Eugene N. Anderson, *Nationalism and the Cultural Crisis in Prussia 1806-1815* (New York: Farrar and Rinehart, 1939).

36

of Italy, in that British rule instead of impeding political unification promoted it and thus paved the way for the present efforts of Hindu national leaders. Moreover, the political unification of India is an essential condition not only for the development of social solidarity, but also for the integration of many widely different regional cultures into a common national culture [20]—an integration which in Italy and Germany preceded political unity.

20. Jawaharlal Nehru, *The Unity of India* (London, 1941).

Right now we are observing the beginning of another attempt to overcome political divisions for the purpose of promoting national solidarity within the wide realm of Islamic religious culture, where during the last century national separatism of the peoples with different secular cultures was slowly growing. At the present time, all the people who share Arabic culture and have a common history, going back centuries before the Koran was written, are recognized by many Arab leaders as constituting one nationality, though this nationality is divided into seven separate, independent states. Judging from the efforts of some of its leaders, it seems probable that sooner or later a lasting political unity will be achieved.

However, this tendency toward a political unification based on a common national culture is not universal. On the contrary, sometimes a politically united people already sharing a common national culture becomes politically divided, and these divisions are accepted by intellectual leaders who initiate the creation of a different national culture within each of them. Such, as we know, is the present trend in Spanish American states. We must remember, of course, that considerable regional differences in culture existed within the vast territory of Central and South America at the time when political independence from Spain was won and that these cultural differences, combined with varying geographic conditions, were important factors in the formation of separate states.

Religious divisions raise different problems than political divisions. For, while the latter can be overcome by an integration of several states into one state or at least by a political federation of states, it is almost impossible to integrate several religious groups with divergent sacred cultures. We mentioned before the well-known failure of Indian leaders to unite Hindus and Moslems. Of course, religious divisions can be eliminated by including within a nationality only members of one religious society and excluding all unbelievers. This is how the ruling groups of Spanish nationality treated the Moslems and Jews before the Reformation and the Protestants after it. But the ideologists of certain other nationalities found a different solution. Instead of eliminating religious divisions, they tried to prevent conflicts between them by promulgating the ideal of religious freedom and mutual tolerance as essential for the realization of the common goal of national peace and unity. This ideal became fully realized during the nineteenth century in England, France, and America.

Class conflicts have been generally recognized by social thinkers as interfering with national unity, but nationalistic ideologists differ as to the ways in which these conflicts can be overcome. Some eighteenth-century political and moral philosophers, believing that the only way was to eliminate class divisions and class inequalities, promulgated the famous ideal of a society based on the principles of individual "Liberty, equality, fraternity." For the realization of this ideal, a democratic state was at first considered sufficient. Nevertheless, when class divisions and conflicts, rooted in economic inequality, still remained unsolved, social or, more specifically, economic democracy was advocated by many thinkers as essential for the formation of a classless society. Other nationalistic thinkers, however, assumed that class conflicts could be overcome without eliminating class divisions, provided the upper-class members who formed the elite of a national society functioned as benevolent rulers, using their superior wisdom and power for the guidance, protection, and welfare of the lower classes.

2. *The ideal of national progress.* The general concept

38

of *human progress* was fully developed by philosophers of the eighteenth century; but it had earlier roots in positive valuations of the many cultural innovations which had been accumulating at an increasingly rapid rate from the thirteenth century on. Of these innovations, the growth of new national cultures was the most obvious and the most highly valued by the intellectual leaders who participated in it.

Thus, thinkers who believed in the creative ability of their own nationality, as manifested in its historical past and its present growth, saw still greater possibilities in its future achievements. They promulgated the ideal of a continuous progress of their nationality in every realm of culture—literature, art, philosophy, science, technology, economics, law, social organization. Realization of this ideal would depend, of course, upon the active cooperation of present creative leaders and the future emergence of many new leaders in all these realms.

The ideal of national progress became increasingly influential in Europe from the middle of the eighteenth century on, though it was, and still is, opposed in nearly every nationality by a few romanticists who disapprove of recent innovations, idealize their national past, and long for its return. On the other hand, leaders of nationalities judged culturally backward generally accept it in order to show that these nationalities are fully capable of progress and can eventually reach as high a level as more advanced nationalities, if not a higher one. Sometimes, however, a nationality is considered by its leaders to be backward only in certain realms of culture, but equal or even superior to most nationalities in other realms: thus, Japan fifty years ago was considered as needing progress in science, technology, economics, but not in aesthetics, politics, ethics, or religion.

As the creative growth of a national culture increases in range and rapidity, nationalistic ideologists begin to emphasize its progress as a proof of its greatness, even more than its historical heritage. We observe this emphasis in the United

States, but especially in Russia, where propagandists continually try to persuade their audiences that cultural progress in the Soviet Union under Russian leadership is faster, more inclusive, and more genuine than anywhere else.

3. The ideal of a national mission. Relationships between nationalities are, of course, of primary importance, both from the theoretic and from the practical point of view. Later we shall analyze these relationships as dynamic processes of collective interaction. Now we shall briefly survey some beliefs of thinkers to whom their own nationality is supremely valuable as to what the relationships between it and other nationalities *ought* to be.

As national cultures grew, nationalities began to compete with each other for prestige and influence. A nationality whose culture is supposed by its members to be more highly developed than others strives to have its superiority recognized by peoples with presumably inferior cultures and to make them follow its guidance. This competition is similar to the age-old competition between religious groups. Every group which has a well-developed religion with a sacred literature claims to be superior to others, propagates its superiority, and tries to have its religion accepted by people with different religions.

Now, religious leaders who believe that their religion is the supreme or the only true religion usually assume that it is their mission to convert unbelievers. They interpret this mission as an altruistic duty to be performed for the benefit of unbelievers, who have to be guided from error to truth, from evil to good, from damnation to salvation. We find a similar conception among nationalistic ideologists who believe that their own nationality is much superior culturally to others and consequently that its leaders ought to assume the altruistic duty of sharing it with inferior peoples, if these are capable of sharing it; if not, of helping them reach a cultural level which they would be unable to reach by their own efforts. This is a mission, just like the mission of religious leaders.[21]

21. For a first brief survey of the concept of national missions, see Robert Michels, *Der Patriotismus* (Munich, 1929), Chap. II.

40

Such a mission may be carried on by peaceful methods. But if it meets considerable resistance, if those "inferior" peoples refuse to be guided by their "superiors" and try instead to maintain or even to develop their own cultures, nationalistic ideologists often tend to obtain the support of powerful rulers and governmental groups in order to overcome their resistance. We know from the history of ecclesiastical societies that religious leaders also often appealed to powerful rulers for help in converting resistant unbelievers; it was considered better for the latter to be converted by force than not to be converted at all.

Quite a few French nationalistic thinkers, even as early as the reign of Louis XIV, considered French culture superior to others and believed that it should be shared by intellectuals of other nationalities so as to raise the cultural level of all Europe. Many French cultural leaders, with the sponsorship of kings, ministers, and diplomats, accepted this belief and acted accordingly. The mission was rather successful. A French nationalistic historian of the twentieth century wrote a book dealing with this period of French cultural expansion under the title *L'Europe française*.[22] But the success of the mission was due to its peacefulness. When Napoleon attempted to impose French domination upon Europe by force, his attempt provoked the defensive reaction of other nationalities—especially German and Spanish—and stimulated their solidarity against the French.

After the partition of Poland, some Polish mystics developed a semi-religious conception of a Polish mission. The partition was conceived as analogous to the crucifixion of Jesus. After the resurrection, which was bound to come, Poland would assume a mission like that of Christ; it would spread throughout the world the principle of mutual love between nationalities.

The ideal of an Italian mission was conceived in a somewhat similar way by Mazzini.[23] Liberated Italy would become

22. Louis Réau (Paris, 1938).

23. Cf. Gwilym O. Griffith, *Giuseppe Mazzini, Prophet of Modern Europe* (New York: Harcourt, 1932).

41

the center of a world-wide movement for international understanding, peace, and cooperation.

The ideal of a Russian mission began to be formulated toward the end of the eighteenth century, but at first it was connected with exaltation of the Russian Empire as alleged heir of the Byzantine Empire and destined to become a world empire. The ideal eventually became nationalistic rather than political: The Russian people, because of their moral superiority, had the mission of saving mankind from the demoralized and decadent Western civilization. Russification of other nationalities within the empire came to be conceived as a part of this mission. During the last twenty-five years, the Russian nationality has assumed a new mission: that of spreading communism throughout the world for the benefit of all peoples —by peaceful methods, if not resisted; by force whenever necessary.[24]

The ideal of the German national mission has changed in the course of time. Originally, as conceived by idealistic philosophers, it was a mission of leadership; the creative growth of German culture was to become a model for other nationalities.[25] Later, the superiority of German culture implied the duty of German leaders to make inferior peoples share it for their own benefit: it was a high privilege for Poles, Czechs, and other nationalities existing under the dominion of Austria or Prussia to become Germanized. Twentieth-century racial ideologists, however, rejected the possibility of anybody's becoming a real German who was not so hereditarily; admitting inferior people to membership in the German nationality would only contaminate its racial purity and lower its culture. Consequently, the German national mission then became the rule of all the inferior peoples in the world for the ultimate benefit of humanity. These peoples were to serve their German rulers and perform auxiliary functions which the creative German leaders needed to develop further German culture— the supreme achievement of mankind.[26]

24. See Chapter Five.

25. Cf. Robert R. Ergang, *Herder and the Foundations of German Nationalism* (New York: Columbia University Press, 1931).

26. This mission was clearly formulated by Alfred Rosenberg, *Der Mythus des 20 Jahrhunderts;* and Hitler, *Mein Kampf.* Both followed the doctrine of Houston Stewart Chamberlain, *Die Grundlagen des neunzehnten Jahrhunderts* (Berlin, 1899).

Less authoritarian was the nineteenth-century ideal concerning the English—or, rather, the British—national mission. This mission was to be performed exclusively within the British Colonial Empire. Since all the peoples in this empire were culturally backward and poorly organized, it was the altruistic duty of the British rulers to raise their cultural level and to introduce an adequate order. According to some thinkers— e.g., Kipling—it was a duty which would never cease, a permanent "white man's burden," for those peoples were racially inferior, incapable of preserving without British rule the culture and social order introduced by the British. Other thinkers, however, were more optimistic and believed that the British mission was to teach those peoples how to develop their cultures and to maintain order by their own efforts. This latter conception gradually became more influential.

Somewhat similar, but more specialized, is the mission which Americans have recently assumed in trying to convert the Japanese and the Germans to political democracy.

4. The ideal of national independence. National cultures in Europe grew chiefly during the period of continuous and violent struggles for power between political societies. Small political units were becoming integrated into large states with highly centralized governments, stronger states took extensive territories from weaker states by force, and feeble states were incorporated by conquest into powerful states. Throughout these struggles many peoples whose leaders had developed or were beginning to develop distinct national cultures became subjected to the rule of "foreign" governments, which frequently impeded the further development of their cultures or even tried to eliminate them altogether.

Under such conditions, the national leaders of subject peoples promulgated the ideal of complete independence of their nationalities from foreign domination. This ideal, rooted in a positive appreciation of national cultures as original, valuable, and capable of creative growth obviously differs from

43

27. The case of Finland seems to have been different. "Nationalism began to emerge after the separation from Sweden in 1905. It arose primarily from the apprehension . . . among some younger Finns, lest the union with Russia should be followed by an absorption into the Russian Empire. . . . These patriots believed that absorption could be prevented only if the people were set off sharply from Russia by the possession of a distinct national culture": John H. Wuorinen, *Nationalism in Modern Finland* (New York: Columbia University Press, 1931), p. 1.

28. Robert J. Kerner, *Bohemia in the Eighteenth Century* (New York: Macmillan, 1932).

29. C. R. Jurgela, *History of the Lithuanian Nation* (New York: The Lithuanian American Information Center, 1948).

30. Stephen Shumeyko, *Ukrainian National Movement* (New York: United Ukrainian Organizations of the U. S., 1939); Seymour B. Still, "The Ukrainians. Their struggle for National Independence" (manuscript).

mere political separatism. The latter, initiated by *political* leaders, is based on the opposition of a group inhabiting a certain portion of the territory controlled by a sovereign state against domination by the government of this state, irrespective of cultural similarities or differences. The secession of the South from the Union in 1860 is a familiar example.

Here we cannot investigate in detail the emergence of the ideal of national independence among European nationalities, for their histories manifest considerable differences. Sometimes this ideal was connected with a striving for religious independence, as during the Hussite War in Bohemia, the Dutch revolt against Spanish rule, and the Irish rebellion from the time of Cromwell's invasion. If the national culture was already fully developed, this ideal was promulgated immediately after foreign conquest, as in Poland after the Third Partition. In other cases, however, when the development of a national culture had been interrupted, the ideal of national independence did not appear until this development began to be revived.[27] Thus, the ideal of Bohemian independence reappeared when, after a century and a half of Germanization, intellectual leaders started to recreate Czech culture.[28] The ideal of Lithuanian national independence (as distinct from participation of Polonized Lithuanians in the Polish struggle for independence from Russia) did not start until the Lithuanian literary culture began to be revived in the second half of the nineteenth century.[29] Independence became the goal of Ukrainian leaders when a common Ukrainian national literature started to grow, after centuries of interruption, and Ukrainian history and folk culture became exalted.[30]

Notwithstanding these differences, we find that the ideal of independence was sooner or later accepted by intellectual leaders of *every* nationality in Europe, whenever they believed that their efforts to preserve and develop its culture and solidarity were being impeded by foreign rulers. The same ideal, as we know, has more recently spread to the colonial areas conquered by European powers—e.g., India,[31] Indonesia, and, lately, Nigeria.

However, when a foreign government does not obstruct realization of the ideal of national unity and progress, nationalistic leaders may be satisfied with a degree of political autonomy which they consider sufficient for their purposes, as in Wales or French Canada. This is the kind of autonomy which Soviet Russia grants to minor nationalities under its rule—always, of course, under the condition that there will be no resistance against its communist mission.

Historians and ideologists have been influential in making other creative leaders conscious of the continuity of cultural growth, by emphasizing the dependence of their present achievements upon the past achievements of their predecessors and showing their value in opening up the way for future achievements of their successors. Of course, not all creative leaders believe that their main function is to contribute to this continuous growth of their national culture; but that most of them do so believe is, as we shall see, clearly manifested in the formation of many national associations devoted to this common purpose.

The social roles of artists and musicians

To realize the significance of art and music as components of a national culture, we must take into consideration the social aspect of these cultural products. Although they are not so essential as language for the maintenance of social relations between people, yet—as some sociologists pointed out long ago—they do serve in some measure as means of social communication and unification.[32] People who experience, understand, and appreciate a painting, a sculpture, a musical composition share the representations, ideas, and emotions which this aesthetic work expresses.

31. Cf. Amvika Charan Mazumdar, *Indian National Evolution* (Madras, 1917); Chandra Dharma S. Gooneratne, *The Development of Political Consciousness in India, 1757-1931* (Chicago: privately published University of Chicago thesis, 1936); William Roy Smith, *Nationalism and Reform in India* (New Haven: Yale University Press, 1938); Bruce Tiebout McCully, *English Education and the Origins of Indian Nationalism* (New York: Columbia University Press, 1940); W. E. Duffett, *India Today; the Background of the Indian Nationalist Movement* (Toronto, 1941).

32. E.g., Jean Marie Guyau, *L'Art au point de vue sociologique*, 7th ed. (Paris, 1906).

Art and music are found in practically all traditional cultures which have been studied by ethnologists, though they vary in different tribal and folk communities. Art is usually connected with the decoration of technical products, music with poetry and dancing. Both often have a magico-religious significance.

With the development of literary religious cultures, specialized professional roles of artists and musicians evolved. Architects planned temples and guided the workers who built and decorated them, sculptors and painters made images of mythical beings and representations of mythical events; musicians participated in religious ceremonies. Because their products had a sacred meaning, they either were priests themselves or, as religious cultures became increasingly complex, their functions were controlled by priests, and their performances required the guidance of specialists.

The early artists and musicians integrated in their creative works components derived from different traditional cultures, and consequently common patterns of sacred art and sacred music extended over more or less wide regions with different traditional cultures and persisted for a long time. We know little about Egyptian music, but the sacred art of Egypt can be identified and distinguished by its basic patterns. The religious art and music of the Greek Orthodox Church, developed and stabilized in Byzantium, spread widely, underwent some creative innovations, especially in Russia, but preserved considerable uniformity. The art and music of the Roman Catholic Church expanded over several continents; though in consequence of the regional variations due to widely different folk cultures and the many creative innovations introduced throughout the centuries, they manifest less uniformity than those of other religions. Yet certain basic standards and norms are universally applied.

But, however influential religious art and music became in Europe after the spread of Christianity, it has never been all-

46

inclusive. Much of the folk art and folk music remained outside of the realm of organized religion and preserved a definitely secular character. Moreover, some products of the secular art of classical antiquity survived and could be used as models. Professional artists gradually ceased to depend entirely on the patronage of priests, as they gained the sponsorship of kings, nobles, heads of republican governments, military leaders, wealthy capitalists. Eventually, the agglomerated works of the men who partly followed the models left by Greek and Roman artists and partly used some patterns of folk art resulted in the creative growth of a national art. Later, secular national music developed, mainly from folk music.

The creative growth of Italian art from the beginning of the Renaissance is a good example. It was "Italian" in the sense that it was developed by artists born and brought up in Italy, sharing the Italian language, apprenticed under the guidance of Italian masters, and continuing the creative work of their predecessors. There was no separation between their religious and their secular functions; the same artists could produce works with religious or with secular content. But the aesthetic pattern of their works, even of those produced for the Church, was influenced by secular classical patterns, in opposition to medieval patterns. This does not mean that they remained mere imitators; their originality was steadily increasing. And considerable differences were noticeable between the products of artists trained in various Italian cities—Florence, Pisa, Milan, Turin, Venice, Genoa, Rome. Nevertheless, they had enough in common to have their important creative contributions recognized and appreciated throughout all Italy. Some of them also traveled and worked in several cities; some had disciples and continuators in various areas. Finally, students of art, beginning with Vasari,[33] who were acquainted with the agglomerated contributions of Italian artists, living and dead, to painting, sculpture, architecture, recognized that together they had created an original Italian art, different from

33. Giorgio Vasari, *Lives of the Most Eminent Painters, Sculptors and Architects,* many editions in Italian and in translations, the best being supplemented by later evidence.

47

and superior to every other. This recognition was not limited to Italian connoisseurs; during the sixteenth century in most countries of Western and Central Europe, Italian art was considered supreme, and powerful patrons made it possible for Italian architects, sculptors, painters to function as creators and leaders.

Somewhat later, the agglomerated creative works of professional secular artists who shared other European cultures—French, Spanish, Dutch, German, English—became recognized by the artists themselves, their followers and patrons, as well as by connoisseurs and historians, as constituting original national arts which could be distinguished from each other by definite characteristics. Not all the differences, however, were due to their aesthetic patterns or "styles." Sometimes paintings differ even more by their subject matter. Thus, artists painted mostly landscapes and the people of their own country; this made their work different from that of artists in other countries, and it was easier to achieve this kind of distinction than to create a new original style. Moreover, such works had greater popular appeal; they were more understandable and attractive to the public than works dealing with unfamiliar subjects. The popularity of Dutch art in the seventeenth century is a typical example.

This is why, in countries where original national art was still undeveloped, artists who were aware of the importance of art as a component of national culture and a source of national prestige usually began by painting subjects different from those which foreign artists had been painting. Thus, Polish secular painting, which had been influenced since the Renaissance by Italian artists, became distinctly "national" at the end of the eighteenth century, partly because professional artists incorporated some components of folk art, but mainly because they began to paint Polish landscapes and Polish people and later composed paintings which represented important events of Polish history and Polish national heroes.

48

American professional painters up to the last quarter of the nineteenth century followed the aesthetic patterns of European "schools," first mostly English, later mostly French and German. The distinctive character of their works was due to their content derived from American landscapes and American folk life. Quite a few self-educated artists possessed some individuality, but their works did not initiate any new aesthetic patterns.[34] However, during the last fifty years, aesthetically original works created by American artists, independently of Europe, multiplied.[35]

In Latin American countries, purposive efforts to develop national art began about the same time as efforts to develop national literature. Originality in style, as well as in subject matter, was achieved when artists integrated European aesthetic patterns with old Indian patterns, as Diego Rivera did in Mexico.[36]

Of course, growing innovation by artists of the same nationality and growing communication and interaction between artists of different nationalities make it increasingly difficult for aesthetes to classify all the works of art produced at a given period as components of separate and distinct national cultures. But it is not the competent judgment of the aesthete which matters from the sociological point of view. What is important is the belief of the artists themselves, their followers, patrons, and the public that most, if not all, of the works of these artists constitute a national art, a vast and growing complex of aesthetic values common to all participants in their culture.

A comparative survey of the origin of modern professional secular music has led many musicologists to the conclusion that it emerged from folk music.[37] The distinctive character of folk music which composers of particular nationalities found in their own culture areas and used in their compositions was the primary source of the differences between their works which were intended to be and eventually became recognized as parts of their national cultures. Of course, this was not the only basis

34. Nevertheless, some originality appeared, due to the influence of folk art: Esther Shulman, "How Folk Art made up National Art in the United States and in Japan" (manuscript).

35. See, e.g., Holger Cahill and Alfred H. Barr, eds., *Art in America* (New York: Reynal and Hitchcock, 1934); Talbot F. Hamlin, *The American Spirit in Architecture* (New Haven: Yale University Press, 1926); Sadakichi Hartmann, *A History of American Art*, 2 vols. (New York: Tudor, 1934).

36. Cf. *Contemporary Art in Latin America* (Washington, D. C.: Pan-American Union, Division of Intellectual Cooperation, 1945).

37. Cf. Carl Engel, *An Introduction to the Study of Nationalist Music* (London, 1865); Robert Michels, *op. cit.*

38. Ralph Vaughan Williams, *National Music* (London, 1935).

39. Hans Engel, *Deutschland und Italien in ihren musikgeschichtlichen Beziehungen* (Regensburg, 1947).

40. Aaron Copland, *Our New Music* (New York: McGraw, 1941); Deana Levin, "Nationalistic Music" (manuscript); Carla Heiss, "The Development of National Music in Germany and the United States" (manuscript).

of their differences. The fact that professional musicians were mostly taught by musicians of their own nationality and continued the creative work of their predecessors contributed to the growth of distinctive national music.[38] This is, for instance, why Italian music and German music have remained different in some basic respects in the course of their development from the beginning of the eighteenth century on.[39]

We shall mention only a few well-known examples of composers who purposely initiated and continued the development of national music: Chopin and Moniuszko, Dvorak and Smetana, Glinka and Rimsky-Korsakov, Grieg and Ole Bull, Sibelius. All of them used the folk music of their respective nationalities—Polish, Czech, Russian, Norwegian, Finnish. The recent emergence of American national music from folk music is another and familiar example.[40]

Furthermore, the national significance of music has been considerably enhanced by its connection with themes derived from folklore and national literature—mythology, story, epic, drama, even history. Take, e.g., Wagner's *Meistersinger* and *Nibelungen,* Glinka's *A Life for the Tsar,* Borodin's *Prince Igor,* Mussorgsky's *Boris Godunov,* Sibelius' use of themes from *Kalevala.*

Of course, nowadays any prominent work in the realm of music, just as in architecture, painting, and sculpture, can influence the creative leaders of many nationalities.

The social roles of scientists

Here we use the term "scientists" with a broad meaning to denote not only specialists in certain realms of knowledge—mathematicians, astronomers, physicists, chemists, biologists, and so-called "social scientists"—but also general theorists, now usually called "philosophers." Originally there was no fundamental distinction between their functions, as far as the development of national cultures was concerned. Galileo, Descartes, Newton, Leibnitz, and even Spencer were philosophers, as well as scientists, in the present sense of those terms. Only the functions of "philosophers of values," especially of social philosophers who formulated ethical and political ideals, were different from the functions of scientists. Furthermore, since until recently no clear distinction was made between theoretic and applied science, many scientists from the sixteenth century on were also, or even primarily, inventors and later engineers who planned and organized the practical applications of inventions.

At first most of the creative works of modern European scientists, being written in Latin, were not considered parts of national cultures, any more than the works of the medieval scholars. However, they were more independent of religious doctrines. We know what strong opposition on the part of the Church those scientists met whose theories contradicted or were supposed to contradict doctrines accepted by theologians as absolutely true. Some of them were treated as heretics and rebels against divinely instituted authority. Reading their works was prohibited; they could not transmit their knowledge to the younger generation by regular teaching, since the universities as public centers of higher education were controlled by the Church. Nonetheless, the theories of these scientists spread, and their contributions to knowledge agglomerated. This was partly due to the influence of Humanism, partly to the fact that many apparently minor scientific discoveries seemed irrelevant to the established doctrines. In any case, quite a few scientists obtained support from powerful secular patrons, and most of them gained adherents, disciples, and collaborators by private intercourse—direct personal contacts and/or correspondence.

Of course, patronage was granted primarily to those whose work was expected to be useful to their patrons, and whatever theoretic work they did seemed of little interest unless it could be proved important for the practical purposes of the patrons. In the long run, nonetheless, such patronage did promote the development of science, as, e.g., the history of astronomy shows. As late as the seventeenth century, Kepler stated that most of the help which astronomers needed for their scientific studies was obtained from patrons who wanted them to function as astrologers.[41] Likewise, in more recent times, the sponsorship of inventions by industrial corporations has contributed to the development of scientific research.

It was usually easier for scientists to gain patrons, followers, and collaborators among people who used their language and were conscious of belonging to the same nationality, although there were some notable exceptions. Moreover, readers who were not professional scholars, but amateurs, could understand scientific works better if written in their national language rather than in Latin. Therefore, from the seventeenth century on, scientific literature was increasingly written and published in the popular languages.

The main reason, however, why scientific works gradually came to be considered as parts of national cultures was the steady, rapid growth of modern science and its recognition by intellectuals as one of the most important human achievements. A national culture society gained prestige whenever its scientists contributed to the advancement of scientific knowledge. Consequently, historians began to extol the past achievements of scientists of their own nationality, and ideologists assumed that new scientific achievements were essential for future national progress.

We are familiar with the significant distinction which has arisen between the *duties* of scientific theorists and those of scientific inventors toward their national societies. While a theorist is supposed to make his theories accessible to foreign scientists for the sake of national prestige, an inventor is usually expected to make his inventions available first, or even exclusively, to the technological planners and organizers of his own

41. Bigourdan, *L'Astronomie* (Paris, 1917).

52

nationality, if and insofar as their use will increase its economic or political power.

The social roles of economic leaders

The development of modern commerce and banking and the advancement of material techniques from individual craftsmanship to collective industrial production obviously depended upon political conditions and in turn influenced political societies. Thus, commerce and transportation were conditioned by the territorial divisions within and between states and subjected to the control of governments; governments also could, and did, control industrial production within their territories. On the other hand, state finances depend upon taxes and loans. This connection between political and economic systems has engaged almost exclusively the attention of political and economic historians; relatively little attention has been paid to the connection between economic development and the growth of national culture societies.

This may have been partly due to the early conception of the "economic man." Private capitalists in general—merchants, bankers, industrial entrepreneurs, promoters, and leaders of corporations—were conceived as "economic men" par excellence, motivated by the desire for profit and successful insofar as their actions were rationally planned in conformity with the general laws formulated by economic theorists. Undoubtedly, in performing their specific roles they did act in accordance with this conception. But they also belonged to various social groups and as members were expected to conform with the standards and norms of those groups; consequently, their roles as members affected their roles as capitalists, and vice versa.

Thus, membership in a religious society exerts a considerable influence upon economic roles. For centuries the primary duty of Jewish economic leaders in the Diaspora has been to cooperate with their fellow members for the common interest of their society. The economic influence of the Parsis in India is also the result of religious solidarity.

National economic solidarity was first noticeable between merchants of the same nationality who were trading abroad with "foreigners." Thus, the economic cooperation of the maritime cities included in the Hanseatic League was in some measure due to the fact that the merchants in most of those cities were Germans. Somewhat later the merchants of Dutch maritime cities became increasingly united for the purposes of foreign trade. French merchants of the fifteenth century, in trading with the Near East, were quite solidary in their competition with Italian merchants, as is shown by the biography of the most famous French merchant of that period, Jacques Coeur, a prominent French patriot.[42] The expansion of European trade after the discovery of maritime routes by which direct contacts with Far Eastern peoples could be established increased the growing solidarity of merchants of the same nationality—Portuguese, Spanish, English, Dutch, French—both in relations with oriental natives and in competition with other European nationalities. A famous example of national solidarity which has lasted through centuries is that of Scottish businessmen abroad. We recently heard much about the strong national bonds which united German businessmen in Latin America and which the Nazi regime tried to use for its imperialistic purposes.

On the other hand, no such solidarity was expected between merchants who initiated and carried on trade within a territory inhabited by people of their own nationality; competition among them was considered normal. Nevertheless, with the growth of national consciousness the idea emerged that they were actually performing functions which contributed toward national unification. They helped overcome local and regional separatism by making accessible to inhabitants of every area the products of inhabitants of other areas. Moreover, they had

42. Albert B. Kerr, *Jacques Coeur, Merchant Prince of the Middle Ages* (New York: Scribner, 1927).

considerable influence in promoting the expansion of public roads and the invention and use of new means of transportation. The recognition of these functions as important for national unification was well manifested in the efforts of nationalistic leaders to eliminate such obstacles to trade and transportation as the tariffs imposed by local and regional governments on the importation of goods produced by people belonging to the same nationality but inhabiting other regions. For instance, the elimination of the economic separatism of German states preceded the political unification of Germany.

Most significant, however, from the sociological point of view is the growing influence of the ideal of national solidarity upon the roles of the capitalists who sponsor inventors, the technological planners, and the organizers whose rapidly agglomerating contributions have resulted in the creative growth of modern industry. Capitalists have provided the necessary means of industrial production—including "labor"—and distributed the products. Without them, the growth of industry would have depended entirely on governmental sponsorship, and we know that until recent times governmental control often impeded rather than promoted industrial innovations, except those which were sure to be useful for military or administrative purposes. This was one of the main justifications of the "laissez faire" doctrine: "free enterprise," independent of governmental interference, was considered essential for industrial progress.

But this justification did not satisfy those social ideologists who wished to eliminate class conflicts as obstacles to national unity. The emergence of a new class hierarchy with capitalists at the top and workers at the bottom was as objectionable to them as the preservation of the old class hierarchy—even more so, for industrial workers had socially less in common with capitalists than the peasants with the gentry.[43] And, since the low economic status of workers invalidated the optimistic doctrine of certain economists that the industrial progress due to

43. Cf. Harry W. Laidler, *A History of Socialist Thought* (New York: Crowell, 1927).

free enterprise would automatically benefit everybody, ideologists of national progress demanded a new type of economic leadership.

Whether as a result of their demand or not, a new type of leader did emerge—the labor leader, who aimed to have workers share the benefits of industrial progress. And, on the other side, the capitalistic leaders of several nationalities gradually became aware of the importance of this ideological issue. English, French, German, Italian, and American capitalists have explicitly or implicitly accepted the idea that it is their duty to raise the economic level of all the people who belong to their national society, and they claim that they are effectively performing this duty.[44] This claim is denied by communist, revolutionary leaders, who insist that capitalists have no other interest but the maintenance of their class supremacy. Therefore, wherever communists gain supreme political control, they take over as public functions all the economic functions hitherto privately performed, but proclaim the idea that the primary duty of economic leaders is to promote the economic progress of their own nationality for the benefit of all its members.

Thus, the majority of modern economic leaders, just like literary, artistic, scientific, and technological leaders, are functioning on behalf of their national culture society, whatever the regime of the political society of which they are members. A few of them act as leaders in international cooperation; but this is a function which will be discussed later.

44. Capitalists' recognition of their social duties is discussed by Werner Sombart, *Der Bourgeois; zur Geistesgeschichte des modernen Wirtschaftsmenschen* (Munich-Leipzig, 1913), especially Chap. VIII, "Bürgerliche Tugenden," and Chap. XVII, "Die Philosophie." However, in his main work *Der moderne Kapitalismus* (Munich-Leipzig, 1928), he rather neglects the connection between capitalism and nationalism.

three

Social groups functioning

on behalf of national culture societies

Social centers of cultural leaders

During the early stages of the development of national cultures, the cultural leaders and their followers who contributed to it were not well organized, although some of them did congregate temporarily or permanently in social centers, where they usually obtained the support of influential patrons.

The first of these centers were the *courts of rulers,* and they remained rather important until recent times. In the twelfth and thirteenth centuries, the courts of Provence were centers where the local literature flourished. In Italy from the fifteenth century on, the court of the Medici in Florence, that of the Sforzas in Milan, in some measure the smaller courts (the court of Urbino, as described by Castiglione),[1] and finally the Papal court in Rome were during certain periods centers where Italian men of letters, historians, and artists congregated. The royal court of France began to function as the main center of French men of letters under Francis I and under Louis XIV became the most influential cultural center in history. In England, the cultural influence of the royal court fluctuated with the changing dynasties. In Germany, some smaller courts— Saxony, Bavaria, Weimar—did more during some periods to promote the development of German culture than the imperial court of Vienna, though not until the middle of the nineteenth century did the Prussian court become important from the cultural point of view. In Russia, on the contrary, the imperial court was the original and remained for more than a hundred years the most influential center of Russian culture.

Of course, the patronage of rulers was seldom altruistic. As, with the decay of the feudal system, rulers became the administrative, legislative, and juridical heads of their states, a secular literary language was recognized as essential for the performance of their functions. Authors of epics, dramas, lyrical poetry, as well as historians, were favored if in their works they praised the ruler and his achievements or exalted his ancestors; and

1. Baldassare Castiglione, *Il Cortegiano* (Florence, 1894).

58

from a purely aesthetic point of view all their works were supposed to contribute to the prestige of their patrons. Artists were expected to build and adorn the palaces of rulers, so as to make them as beautiful and magnificent as those of other rulers, if not more so, and to perpetuate in flattering portraits and statues the persons of the rulers, their wives, and their children. Musicians composed music for public ceremonies at court, military music, and sometimes the music for songs and operas exalting rulers, present or past.

Another kind of center for the gathering of cultural leaders was the autonomous *city,* and in the course of time it became much more important than the court. Many cities, indeed, from earliest times, contained centers of religious culture; and if they were the capitals of monarchical states, the courts of the rulers continued to function as secular centers. But this was not why cities exerted an increasing influence upon the development of national cultures. It was rather because, in the first place, they had an organization of their own, including social groups with special functions—craftsmen's guilds, associations of tradesmen, local governmental groups, etc.; and, in the second place, because as economic centers they were continually growing in size, wealth, and complexity. In the course of this growth, an increasing number of wealthy merchants, bankers, nobles, and people with higher education—lawyers, physicians, university professors—came to reside within their limits.

Consequently, in these autonomous cities creative leaders in all realms of national cultures found followers and sponsors who made them in some measure independent of the patronage and control of sovereign rulers; and, as travel and communication between the cities increased, this independence grew. Especially important in the latter respect, as we know, was the invention of the printing press, which made the works of writers, musical compositions symbolized on paper, etchings and engravings, reproductions of paintings, drawn or painted representations of buildings, sculptures, technical products, animals and plants, geographical maps, etc., easily and widely accessible.

From the sociological point of view, the most important result of the growth of urban centers was the steady development of organized groups or associations functioning in order to promote the creative development and expansion of national cultures. The most famous of such associations were called "academies," after the Platonic Academy, which was mainly an association of philosophers, but the term "academy" came to be used with various other meanings.[2]

2. For a good, though brief, survey of academies, see *Encyclopaedia Britannica* (1949).

Associations of men of letters

Italy in the sixteenth and seventeenth centuries was remarkable for the number of its literary academies, but the best known and most influential literary association in history is the *Académie française*. Beginning as a small and informal group of men of letters living in Paris, it was institutionalized under the sponsorship of Richelieu, and during the reign of Louis XIV the selection of its members and its functions became officially regulated. Since then it has remained almost changeless, whether sponsored by kings, emperors, or republican governments. Its basic tasks are: first, to maintain perpetually the high aesthetic standards of French literature by selecting for its limited membership of "forty immortals" the best creative authors; second, to normalize the use of the French language by periodically listing and defining newly recognized words in a dictionary and by formulating grammatical rules.

The *Académie française* has served as a model for central literary associations of other European countries, whether called "academies" or not, whether under the patronage of rulers (as in Prussia and Russia) or without such patronage. However, in each country, as the number of men of letters in-

60

creased and as aesthetic innovations grew, the exclusiveness of such an elite and its conservative tendencies inevitably led to the formation of other associations less exacting as to the status of their members and more willing to recognize new patterns of literary work.

Nowadays, wherever original national literature has begun to develop, associations promoting this development are organized.[3] Thus, in the United States, the American Academy of Arts and Letters was founded in 1904; several literary associations have been founded in every Latin American country [4] and recently in Canada.[5] Particularly interesting is the All-Indian Centre which was founded in 1934 and included nearly 300 leading Indian writers, with Rabindranath Tagore as president. Since there is not one, but many Indian literatures, sacred and secular, written in different languages, the purpose of this association is to contribute to national unity by stimulating common appreciation of all of them.[6]

It is not usually the function of a literary association to promote the spread of national literature. Other groups soon begin to perform this task; groups of printers and publishers which make all kinds of literary works accessible to thousands of readers, libraries, book stores, theatrical companies playing dramatic works before audiences which can understand the spoken national language, and finally various readers' clubs.

For a long time, however, one important function in the realm of aesthetic literature was not performed by any organized group: that of teaching future writers how to use a national language in producing literary works. This function was originally performed by individual teachers, since the schools of higher education, which in the Middle Ages were under the control of priests, taught only Latin and even after the Renaissance continued to neglect modern national languages. Although for purely practical purposes reading and writing in the vernacular began to be taught quite early in some urban schools on a low level, it was still considered unworthy of being

3. In Ireland, the tendency to separate Irish culture from English culture by reviving Gaelic language and literature was stimulated by the Gaelic League of Dublin, whose proceedings and works have been published since 1870.

4. For instance, by 1949 twenty-one such associations had been organized in Brazil, and nine in Argentina: Dorothy Olson, "Literature and Literary Associations in Argentina and Brazil" (manuscript).

5. With the explicit purpose of promoting the growth of an original Canadian culture and the national solidarity of the Canadian people: Sylvia Truster, "The Canadian Authors' Association" (manuscript).

6. The *India and Pakistan Yearbook and Who's Who*, 1950, p. 516.

taught in universities to future scholars, so long as national literatures were held inferior to classical Latin and Greek literatures. Only when national literatures grew in wealth and became recognized by influential critics as aesthetically valuable and original did university professors begin to impart knowledge and appreciation of these literatures to their students and help them to master their national language.

Associations for the promotion of knowledge

Many local Italian academies from the fifteenth century on included not only men of letters contributing to Italian literature, but also classical scholars, philosophers, historians, and later natural scientists—among them the academies of Florence, Turin, Lucca, Naples, Palermo. Only in 1878 was a National Academy organized in Italy. In England, the Royal Society, founded in the seventeenth century, also came to include philosophers, scientists, and scholars with various specialties.

In France, some thirty years after the foundation of the literary *Académie française,* an *Académie des sciences* was organized from an informal association of scientists and philosophers. After a century and a half of changes and additions, the French Institute finally evolved as a central association with two main divisions: one for mathematicians, astronomers, physicists, chemists, and biologists; the other for historians, "moral" and "political" scientists, and philosophers. From the beginning of the eighteenth century on, academies of sciences were founded in other European countries under the sponsorship of kings or emperors. For instance, a *Preussische Akademie der Wissenschaften* was founded in Berlin, a *Bayerische Akademie der Wissenschaften* in Munich, an *Akademie der Wissenschaften* in Vienna, and a Royal Academy in Denmark. In Russia at the time of the Bolshevik Revolution, the *Imperial Academy of Sciences* was nearly two hundred years old; its name was then changed, but it continues to function as before, with primary emphasis on physical sciences and mathematics, but also with some consideration for Russian language, literature, and history.

On the other hand, quite a few academies and similar associations under different names were privately organized. Thus, the Polish Academy in Cracow and the Czechish Academy in Prague were founded in the nineteenth century without the sponsorship of the Austrian emperors. The American Philosophical Society in Philadelphia, which comprises all departments of learning, was also privately founded in 1740 and chartered by the General Assembly of Philadelphia in 1780. The National Academy of Sciences in Washington, D.C., was incorporated by Congress in 1863.

Now, the main purpose of these scientific academies was to promote the development of knowledge in general within their own national culture societies. To a certain degree the academies of Vienna, Munich, and Berlin competed with each other, since each aimed primarily to promote knowledge within the political society ruled by its own sponsor; but this did not interfere with their common purpose of stimulating the growth of German science, any more than the competition of literary or musical associations in several cities of the same nationality interferes with the development of their common national literature or music.

The nationalistic purpose of most of these associations was clearly manifested in the exclusion of foreigners from active membership, especially during the nineteenth century. As we shall see later, prominent foreign scientists were often invited to participate in intellectual intercourse, but they had no share in the organization of these groups.

In selecting scientists of their own nationality for membership, most of these academies follow, though not so consistently, the principle used by the *Académie française* in selecting authors for membership. They aim to form a small elite of the best scientists. To be admitted to full membership, a scientist must have already proved by his superior achievements that he is worthy, according to the judgment of the active members, who themselves belong to the elite. Of course, the explicit justification for this principle is to maintain high intellectual standards among the scientists of their nationality. Whatever the members of this association do, individually or collectively, in any branch of knowledge is supposed to serve as a model for others. And the theory is that, since being admitted to membership gives considerable prestige, competition for this prestige will stimulate good scientific work. However, as a consequence of the selection of older men who have already completed their main work in a well-standardized realm of knowledge, academies often become rather conservative. For instance, when sociology began to develop, it was kept waiting a long time for recognition from the academies.

Associations of specialists in particular realms of knowledge

As the function of academies in promoting the development of knowledge became less and less satisfactory to the majority of scientists, because of their authoritarianism and their unwillingness to recognize innovations, and as the number of scientists increased and their gradual specialization resulted in the rapid growth of innovations in every realm of knowledge, many associations of specialists were organized. They were—and still are—rather democratic, including all the scientists with professional preparation and even amateurs in the same speciality; and most of them not only recognize, but purposely encourage, innovations.[7]

From the very first, natural scientists formed separate associations, which did not include scholars, i.e., specialists in what were later called social sciences and humanities, and these asso-

7. Many of these associations, as we know, publish periodicals which include contributions of their members and reports about their collective functions.

64

ciations became increasingly differentiated. By the second half of the nineteenth century, distinct associations of astronomers, physicists, chemists, botanists, zoologists, and geographers had been organized, and further divisions have been emerging since then. Special associations of social scientists and humanists began to evolve a little later, and at the beginning of this century we already find separately organized groups of historians, philologists, ethnographers and anthropologists, political scientists, economists, psychologists, sociologists. In the course of this evolution, almost everywhere associations of philosophers were formed separately, since philosophy became definitely distinguished from science. To counteract this separatism, some attempts were made to integrate partially many associations into a more general one, as exemplified by the American Association for the Advancement of Science.[8] In India, the emergence of many specialized learned societies led to a promulgation of the ideal of their integration as a method of promoting cultural unity and solidarity.[9] An attempt at a different kind of integration started recently in Poland. The Congress of Polish Science, which met in June, 1951, was intended to initiate the cooperation of all Polish scientists and scientific associations for the realization of socialism (= communism) in Poland.

All the associations which were mentioned above are primarily devoted to the development of theoretic knowledge. Although there is no sharp division between theoretic science and applied science, yet, since the social roles of scientists who specialize in research obviously differ from the social roles of those who use the results of this research for practical purposes, we find also associations of professional specialists who apply scientific knowledge in practice. Medical associations and associations of jurists were the first to evolve, probably because medicine and law have for centuries been recognized as scientific disciplines, taught in universities in preparation for practical functions. Associations of the professional engineers who

8. Cf. Ralph Samuel Bates, *Scientific Societies in the United States* (New York: J. Wiley & Sons, 1945, Chap. III).

9. Elizabeth Dressel (manuscript); Kewal Motwani, *Science and Society in India* (Bombay, 1945).

10. Leonard H. Stidley wrote a historico-comparative survey of these associations in Britain and the United States (unpublished Master's thesis, University of Illinois, 1951).

had been scientifically trained in technological schools started to develop in the last quarter of the nineteenth century.[10] Somewhat later, after businessmen—merchants, entrepreneurs, bankers—who previously had been trained by apprenticeship, or by self-education through trial-and-error techniques, had learned in business schools some results of the scientific research carried on by economists and others, and had been taught to apply these results to practical problems, professional or semi-professional associations of businessmen were organized: chambers of commerce, associations of manufacturers, Rotary Clubs, etc. And when scientific research came to be applied in planning and testing such social activities (hitherto performed by traditional methods) as education and social work, individuals who specialized in these activities organized groups which were intended primarily to deepen and enlarge their scientific foundations.

Now, such associations are likely to differ, not only because they are composed of specialists in various branches of knowledge, but also in other respects. Thus, some of them are local or provincial; others are federations of local groups; still others have individual members scattered over a wide territory. Some, especially those of businessmen, use their knowledge primarily (though not exclusively) for the benefit of their own members; others (e.g., medical or educational associations) primarily for the benefit of large numbers of outsiders. But there are important similarities underlying their differences. First, the majority of them, like the old academies, formally or informally limit their active membership to individuals of their own nationality. Second, nearly all of them explicitly or implicitly function to promote the development of knowledge, theoretic or applied, *within their own national society*. In a later chapter we shall discuss the trends toward cultural cooperation which have been developing between scientists of different nationalities.

The national function of universities

The main function of universities as organized groups of professors and students is, of course, educational. Their task is to prepare students for various socially important roles by having professors impart to them the kind and amount of knowledge that they will need for the performance of such roles. The majority of these roles will be performed outside the universities; but a selected minority of students are being prepared for the roles of university professors, and these will eventually succeed the professors who prepared them and continue to impart to future students whatever knowledge the latter will need.

When education is the only function of a university, this obviously means that the university is not intended to promote the creative growth of knowledge, but merely to perpetuate the knowledge that is already developed and shared by its professors. Such was the explicit task of most medieval universities. There theology, law, medicine, or philosophy (which was a residual category for the generalized knowledge not integrated into the other three branches) were taught by professors who were supposed to possess all the "true" knowledge in these realms and to transmit it to their successors. Additions by professors to existing knowledge were allowed, if proved to be consistent with the established "absolutely true" doctrines, especially the theological doctrines.

However, as knowledge gradually became secularized and specialization increased, universities began to include on their faculties specialists in various realms of secular knowledge which had not been taught before. But not until any new specialty gained the recognition and the support of scientific associations were university faculties willing to include it among the subjects taught and to admit its leaders as professors. Specialists in classical studies came first; and we have already noticed how the prestige of these studies delayed the

recognition of modern national literatures and their acceptance as academic subjects. Higher mathematics met no opposition, since some mathematics had always been taught by the
faculty of philosophy. Astronomy and physics began to be introduced toward the end of the eighteenth century; chemistry
and later biology, about the middle of the nineteenth. And the
organized professional training of historians in universities
started in the first half of the nineteenth century.

With this growing specialization, philosophy became gradually limited, although not until the last quarter of the nineteenth century was psychology recognized as a distinct academic discipline, instead of merely a part of philosophy.
Whereas political science and law had originally been combined, political science slowly became accepted by most universities as a separate subject. Economics gained recognition
from university faculties toward the end of the nineteenth century, cultural anthropology only during the twentieth century.
The opposition of European university faculties to the introduction of sociology is perhaps the most conspicuous example
of professorial conservatism.

Further, we must remember that European universities for
a century consistently refused to include applied natural sciences, except medicine with its age-old prestige. Consequently,
separate polytechnical schools, later agricultural schools, still
later business schools, had to be organized. American universities, as we know, were much more liberal in this respect.

However slowly the knowledge taught in universities expanded into new realms, nonetheless, modern universities un-
questionably contributed much to its creative growth. Nowadays, the resistance of faculties to innovations is seldom due to
conflicts with established doctrines dogmatically accepted, but
rather to doubts about the efficiency of the methods used by
innovators and the validity of their results. Faculties still hesi-
tate to take the risk that the work of their members or young
disciples might be proved by critics to be theoretically invalid.

In the course of this penetration of secular knowledge into universities, the latter gradually developed into institutional groups of particular nationalities, unlike the medieval universities, all of which functioned as institutions of the one, "universal" Church.[11] The major educational function of nearly every modern university is to help raise the level of the professional roles performed by educated people of the nationality to which the great majority of its professors and students belong; and in this respect most universities cooperate with the professional associations of practical specialists—physicians, lawyers, engineers, businessmen, etc. The theoretic function of nearly every university is to promote the creative growth of knowledge within its own national culture society by training students for creative work and by offering teaching roles, with rights to economic subsistence, to those who are making or are expected to make significant contributions to this growth. In performing this function universities cooperate with scientific associations of the same nationality. These two nationalistic functions are perhaps best exemplified by French and German universities at the beginning of this century. We shall discuss later some trends toward international cooperation, as when foreigners are invited to function as professors or foreign students are admitted.

11. It is significant that, while we have general histories of medieval universities — e.g., Hastings Rashdall, *The Universities of Europe in the Middle Ages,* new ed., 3 vols. (Oxford, 1936) — no general history of modern universities has been attempted. There are only histories of particular universities, and some works covering the universities of some one nationality—e.g., Friedrich Paulsen, *Geschichte des gelehrten Unterrichts auf den Deutschen Schulen und Universitäten vom Ausgang des Mittelalters bis zur Gegenwart,* 2 vols. (Leipzig, 1896-97), or Maurice J. Caullery, *Universities and Scientific Life in the United States,* trans. by James H. Woods and Emmet Russell (Cambridge: Harvard University Press, 1922).

Artistic and musical associations

The evolution of organized groups of artists was somewhat different from the evolution of literary and scientific associations. Artists, like the craftsmen of the Middle Ages, formed local guilds, and art was taught (sometimes still continues to be taught) by individual masters to a few apprentices. But, as the social roles of artists ceased to be limited to particular urban circles, and prominent artists gained patrons and followers in many cities, even in foreign countries, local guilds could no longer unite or control them. Moreover, with the growth of well-to-do middle classes, which imitated the upper classes in building and decorating their homes and having their portraits painted, an increasing demand arose for the products of artists—architects, sculptors, and especially painters. The slow method of personal apprenticeship then proved insufficient to train the numerous artists needed by the public.

Consequently, super-local associations of professional artists and, somewhat later, professional schools of art began to be organized. Since art was already recognized as a component of national culture, the members of these associations and the teachers in these schools were usually artists of the same nationality. Inasmuch as artistic excellence is one of the sources of national prestige, the chief function of such associations is to maintain high aesthetic standards of national art; therefore, only the best artists are admitted to membership. And the chief task of such schools is to train future artists who will make aesthetically valuable contributions to national art; therefore, the schools select only well-recognized artists as teachers.

The French Académie des Beaux Arts (initiated as early as 1671) and the Royal Academy of Arts in England are well-known associations of the artistic elite. Similar associations exist in other countries, e.g., in Germany, Austria, Russia, Poland, the United States. Some of them started the formation of professional schools of art; most of them cooperate with these schools and often try to influence the selection of their teachers and their methods of teaching. Sometimes they also tend to prevent the competition of foreign artists and to counteract foreign influences. It is significant that until the end of the nineteenth century the works of foreign artists usually were, and occasionally still are, excluded from the exhibitions of artistic works arranged by national associations.

Such closed associations of the artistic elite, especially when they control schools of art, usually become conservative, treat as abnormal aberrants the rebellious artists who initiate new

70

trends conflicting with established styles.[12] The rebels and their followers frequently organize separate artistic associations and try to make the schools of art accept and teach their new aesthetic patterns. If victorious, these rebellious groups in the course of time also become conservative, opposing any further innovations. However, most of the national artistic associations which evolved in the twentieth century remained less exclusive and less conservative than the older ones; consequently the domination of the recognized elite has decreased considerably.

In the realm of music, organized cooperative groups of professionals (orchestras, associations of operatic singers and of musicians), aided by the groups of amateurs who sponsor and support musical performances, have perpetuated the works of composers as parts of national cultures and promoted new compositions.[13] Professional schools of music developed fully during the nineteenth century and almost eliminated individual apprenticeship of young musicians under the guidance of masters. As these schools multiplied, some cooperation between them developed. Thus, in the United States there is a National Association of Schools of Music which includes 196 particular schools. These groups are less nationalistic, more willing to include foreign members, than literary, scientific, or even artistic associations.

12. A typical example was the treatment of impressionist rebels in France.

13. Besides operas and orchestras, we refer here also to associations organized both to promote and spread music and to maintain the status of musicians. There are six such associations in the United States.

Political groups of national ideologists

In our survey of the evolution of national culture societies, we have not yet taken into consideration the influence which this evolution has upon political societies, and vice versa.

We noticed that some of the ideals formulated by national thinkers are intended to produce significant changes in the structure of political societies. Sometimes, indeed, a powerful political ruler may adopt such an ideal and try to realize it. Usually, however, the ideal does not begin to be realized until

71

shared by a number of people who are united and in some degree organized in planning and initiating collective activity. Since they are organized for political purposes, we may call the groups they form "political."

Take, first, the ideal of unification of a politically divided national culture society. We mentioned that this ideal is always promulgated by national thinkers long before, sometimes centuries before, it becomes realized. The ideal of French unification was formulated by Pierre Dubois at the beginning of the fourteenth century, but achieved only at the end of the seventeenth, and then mainly because of its acceptance by a series of powerful rulers of the Kingdom of France, such as Henry IV, Richelieu, Louis XIV. In Italy, however, there was no series of rulers powerful enough to unite all Italy and join to it those parts which were subjected to foreign domination. What we do find from the second half of the eighteenth century on is a growing number of Italian intellectuals gradually organized into associations (like the famous Carbonari) throughout Italy, and later also among Italian emigrants, all of them striving to prepare the way for national liberation and unity. While the final liberation of Lombardy from Austrian domination was due to the Franco-Austrian War under Napoleon III, and it is difficult to ascertain whether and how much these groups influenced the French government, there is no doubt that their influence inside the country did contribute much toward its unification.

After the ideal of German political unity, subordinated for centuries to the ideal of a universal Holy Roman Empire, became distinguished and separated from the latter by nationalistic thinkers in the second half of the eighteenth century and the beginning of the nineteenth, associations of German intellectuals (including university students) became organized to promote its realization. Most of the organizations remained secret, because they combined this ideal with that of a moderate political democracy, opposing the autocracy of the rulers in

72

certain German states. They became sufficiently influential to initiate the struggle of 1848; and, although that struggle failed, nevertheless, their ideals continued to spread among German intellectuals until unification was partially achieved in 1871. The democratic ideal affected in some measure the constitutions of the old German states and of the new German Empire.

The ideal of an egalitarian society of free men voluntarily united under the principle of brotherhood, which French thinkers developed during the eighteenth century, began to be realized only when it was accepted (in combination with somewhat different English ideals) by an informal, but solidary, group of thinkers who participated in the American Revolution and by the organized groups of intellectuals who started the French Revolution. Although it has never yet been fully achieved, we believe that every important step toward its achievement in any society can be proved to have been initiated by a relatively small group of ideologists. The most famous instance of this is the relatively small organized association of Russian intellectuals outside of Russia which, with the aid of still smaller groups of intellectuals within Russia, started to realize the communist variant of this idea—that of a classless society united by the voluntary productive collaboration of all its members. We cannot discuss here the well-known conflict between the ideal itself and the methods of violent struggle for political power which have been used in attempting to achieve it.

Similarly, the ideal of a national mission in relation to other nationalities begins to be realized on the initiative of private groups of intellectuals, even when it requires the active support of powerful governments. Though the conception of the national mission of Tsarist Russia, insofar as military expansion of the empire was concerned, merely exalted the aggressive imperialism of the Russian government, it was not the government, but groups of intellectuals, who after the death of Alexander I initiated the program of Russification of subject

73

nationalities and eventually gained governmental support. Under the communist regime the conflict between Trotzkyites and Stalinists, although obviously a struggle for political power, was rooted in an intellectual conflict between two groups of thinkers, one of which believed that the spreading of communism throughout the world is the task of an international communist organization, the other that it is a Russian national mission. The ideal of the German mission of world supremacy, already implied in Hegel's philosophy of history and explicitly formulated by Houston Chamberlain, was accepted by many intellectuals who gradually gathered around Hitler; it began to be planfully and actively realized after Hitler popularized it in *Mein Kampf* and later came into power.

But the most general and best known private political groups of national ideologists and their followers are those organized for the purpose of planning and achieving national independence from foreign political domination. The usual method of realizing this purpose is violent rebellion—the method which has been used for centuries in struggles against conquerors, tyrants, theocrats imposing their religion by force, domineering social classes. But violent rebellion for the sake of national independence requires considerable social solidarity among the rebels, a devotion to their own nationality strong enough to induce them to risk even their lives for the common cause, as well as efficient political and military leaders.

Social solidarity usually starts among intellectuals who are fully aware of belonging to a national culture society and accept the ideal of national independence as supremely important and absolutely right; these generally include some political leaders able to gain followers among the masses and a few military men capable of organizing and leading rebellious troops.

Most national rebellions are preceded by the formation of private associations of intellectual nationalists. The Polish rebellions provide perhaps the most significant examples. Kosciuszko in 1795 had the support of a "progressive" nationalistic party, composed mainly of educated gentry, some urban professionals, and a few clergymen, most of whom actively participated in the rebellion. The rebellion of 1830, though carried on chiefly by the Polish army, which had been organized for other purposes in the Kingdom of Poland under the rule of Constantine Pavlovich, grand-duke of Russia, as representative of the Tsar, was a result of the striving of the Polish intellectuals for independence not only within the kingdom, but in the territory of the former Grand Duchy of Lithuania. After the defeat, thousands of Polish intellectuals—army officers and civilians—escaped from Poland and organized associations in France, Belgium, and Switzerland, preparing for future rebellions. Another rebellion, started in 1848 as a part of the general European movement for "freedom of the peoples," failed at once; the next one, that of 1863, lasted longer, but also failed.[14]

One of the reasons for the failure of these revolts was that none of them made sufficient appeal to the masses of people to gain enough volunteers; although already under Kosciuszko some peasants joined the rebellious army, their number was quite small. The conditions were different when, at the beginning of World War I, a rebellion against Russia started under the leadership of Pilsudski; for during the preceding fifty years the ideal of national independence had been accepted, not only by intellectuals, but by a large proportion of the workers and the peasants. This acceptance was later fully manifested after the Nazi invasion, when probably no less than two million Poles took an active part in the underground resistance, nearly 200,000 as volunteer soldiers of the underground army.

The Irish rebellions against British rule from 1798 to 1920 were initiated by political associations of intellectual ideologists; [15] and here the size of the rebellious troops depended on the popular appeal and the acceptance of the ideal of independence. Hungarian intellectuals under Kossuth started the 1848

14. This Polish striving for independence from 1795 on was connected with the conviction of leaders that by struggling for their own freedom the Poles were contributing to the freedom of other peoples. Consequently, they tended to cooperate with rebels of other nationalities—Russians against the Tsarist regime, Hungarians, Italians. For expressions of this ideology, see *For Your Freedom and Ours*, eds. Manfred Kridl, Wladyslaw Malinowski, and Józef Wittlin (New York: Frederick Ungar, 1943).

15. Beginning with the Society of the United Irishmen, founded in 1791 under the leadership of Tone, Drennan, and Russell —cf. Frank MacDermot, *Theobald Wolfe Tone* (London, 1939)—and ending with Sinn Fein, one of the most typical groups organized to struggle for national independence— cf. K. M. Henry, *The Evolution of Sinn Fein* (Dublin, 1919).

revolts against Austria. Between 1917 and 1939, the Finnish revolt against Russian domination, the Lithuanian revolts against Russian and Polish domination, the revolt of eastern Ukrainians against Russians and of western Ukrainians against Poles were preceded by the formation of groups of intellectuals who had contributed to the revival of their national cultures and wanted to achieve independence.

However, with the growth in size of modern armies and the tremendous development of military machinery, rebellious groups of volunteers have less and less chance of winning a war against a powerful state, unless they are supported by another powerful state. Consequently, political groups of nationalities striving for independence have been trying to gain such support; and this function has supplemented, eventually supplanted, the function of initiating rebellions. For instance, at the end of the eighteenth century Irish rebels obtained some aid—not very efficient—from the French government, and so did Polish rebels, who joined the Polish Legion which became a part of the French republican army. Later Polish emigrant groups continually, though unsuccessfully, tried to obtain the aid of the French government in their struggle for independence.

It was, of course, relatively easy for nationalistic leaders to gain the support of any strong state which was already involved in political conflict, especially in war, with the state against which their nationality was struggling. Thus, during the many conflicts between the Ottoman Empire and other powers, the latter helped subjugated nationalities within the empire—Greeks, Serbs, Bulgarians, Rumanians—to achieve independence from Turkish rule. We are familiar with the support which Allied powers in the course of World War I gave the Czechs, the Slovaks, and the Southern Slavs in their striving for independence from Austria-Hungary. Each of these nationalities had political groups of intellectuals whose representatives tried to influence directly the governments of France,

76

England, Russia, and the United States. Unofficially they performed functions similar to those of accredited diplomats of
state governments. Masaryk became famous and influential in
this role, for example.

During World War I, Polish political associations had a
more difficult task, for the Poles struggled for independence
from the Russians, who were allies of the Western powers, as
well as from the Germans. Thus, there were two main nationalistic groups, with members in all three parts of Poland as well
as abroad. The group which was primarily anti-Russian and
had started the military revolt against Russia under Pilsudski
originally had the support of Austria, an enemy of the Western powers; whereas the other group, primarily anti-German,
under the leadership of Dmowski gained recognition and support from the Allied governments. This support was gradually
extended to the first group, as conflicts started between it and
the Germans, and definitely after the Bolshevik Revolution,
when Russia ceased to be an ally. It was also the Bolshevik Revolution which led the Western powers to recognize the independence of Lithuania, Latvia, and Estonia.[16]

Right now almost every nationality dominated by the Russians has organized groups of intellectuals among emigrants
abroad which plan for national independence and try to gain
the support of the governments which oppose the expansion of
communist Russia, especially the American government. Recently, for instance, in the United States groups of Ukrainian
intellectuals, as representatives of the only nationality which is
still carrying on guerrilla rebellion against the Soviet Union,
have attempted to induce the American government to send
financial assistance to the rebels.

But the support given by powerful states to foreign nationalities striving for independence is not always due to conflicts
between such states and those against which subjected nationalities are struggling. The principle of national self-determination,
promulgated by Wilson, was not exclusively intended for the

16. To understand fully the
functions of these voluntary
military groups and political
associations struggling for national independence, one must
read, first of all, historical
works written by authors who
belonged to the nationality
which carried on this struggle.
Of course, one cannot rely
upon all the information contained in such works, especially when it concerns the
enemies against whom the society was struggling, but the
essential point is to know
what the struggle meant *from
the point of view of the people
themselves who participated in
it.*

liberation of nationalities subjected to the domination of enemy states. Nor is violent rebellion always a necessary method of achieving independence—the independence of India was finally gained by peaceful methods. The fact is that from the middle of the nineteenth century on, the ideal of national independence, like the ideal of national progress, has been recognized as a *universal* ideal by groups composed of intellectual leaders belonging to many nationalities; and these international groups have been growing in size and influence.

Governmental groups promoting the development of national cultures

We have seen that, from individual roles of cultural leaders who create national cultures and of social thinkers who promulgate national ideals, organized social groups gradually evolve which function on behalf of national culture societies. Similarly, from the roles of individual rulers acting as patrons of cultural leaders, lasting governmental groups evolve which regularly perform these activities.

This evolution may occur under any form of government—autocratic monarchy, constitutional monarchy, democratic republic, dictatorship. What is essential is that the dominant members of the government be sufficiently interested in the cultural advancement of their nationality to use governmental power for the sake of this advancement.

In so doing, they follow the old model of bureaucracy, which originally performed only administrative functions on behalf of the state or the Church. Special permanent groups—"ministries," "departments," "commissariats," etc.—and subgroups of state officials are organized for the purpose of promoting progress, or what they consider progress, in various realms of culture—commerce, banking, industry, agriculture, transportation, communications, natural sciences, theoretic and applied (mostly

78

applied) social sciences, arts, music, literature. Since such groups also require preparation of individuals for future professional roles, some groups of governmental officials eventually take charge of this preparation, assume control of professional schools, obtain state funds for their support, help establish new schools, maintain laboratories, libraries, museums, etc.

At the beginning of this century, such state institutions were perhaps most fully developed in France;[17] but Italy under Fascist rule, Germany under Nazi rule, and especially Soviet Russia far surpassed this development. They have been growing rather slowly in the United States, somewhat more rapidly in England, especially since World War II. The Indian National Congress continually functions to promote Indian culture.[18]

Thus, generally speaking, cultural patronage has shifted from individual rulers to bureaucratic groups; and cultural associations, rather than individual creators, benefit by this patronage. Benefits, however, are conditional—as they were in the past—upon the conformity of those who are patronized with the requirements of the patrons. This inevitably limits creative innovations—as critics of bureaucratic conservatism have always emphasized. Consequently, many cultural associations still avoid, as far as possible, bureaucratic patronage.

However, as we know, considerable differences exist in the degree of control which bureaucratic groups exert and in the range of innovations which they allow. For, especially in democratic countries, they are subjected to political pressure from private associations and sometimes also from public opinion.

17. Cf. Carlton J. Hayes, *France, a Nation of Patriots* (New York: Columbia University Press, 1930).

18. John C. Osoinach, "The Indian National Congress as a Social Group" (manuscript).

four

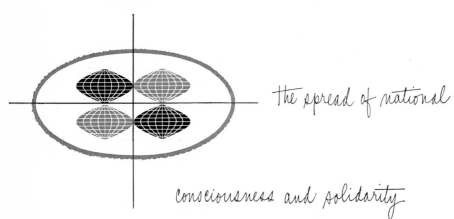

the spread of national

consciousness and solidarity

Intellectuals versus the masses

We find that at a certain stage in the evolution of every national culture society it includes only a relatively small number of intellectuals, who are united by the belief that they belong to a collectivity with a common culture different from
other cultures and who cooperate in perpetuating and developing this culture. They consider themselves Chinese, Italians,
Spaniards, Frenchmen, Englishmen, Germans, Poles, Czechs,
Russians, etc. At first, their social solidarity may not yet be
sufficiently strong to overcome the separatism between them
which is due to the fact that they also belong to other kinds
of social groups with conflicting interests—political, religious,
economic. But it becomes stronger as their common national
culture grows.

These intellectuals also assume that the large masses of
people who apparently share the same culture as they do—
though on a lower intellectual level with many local, regional,
and class variations—belong to the same nationality, are also
Chinese, Italians, Spaniards, Frenchmen, Englishmen, Germans,
Poles, Czechs, Russians, etc., and that consequently they ought
to be solidary, socially united, and socially separated from
peoples with different cultures.

At this stage, however, the assumption is not shared by
the masses of people, most of whom are unconscious of any
common bonds between them over and above the local folk
culture, religion, political allegiance, and class solidarity. For
instance, at the end of the eighteenth century, the majority of
inhabitants of the various regions in Italy, from Piedmont to
Sicily, were unaware that all of them were Italians; and the
masses of people who lived in areas ranging from East Prussia
to the Rhineland and from Hanover to Southern Bavaria did
not think of themselves as being Germans. In Tsarist Russia
during the nineteenth century, in consequence of the strict
hereditary divisions between the classes and the relative isola-

tion of peasant communities, the vast majority of the peasants were utterly unconscious that they were supposed to belong to a Russian society united by a common culture. Even in the twentieth century European peasants in some areas had no idea that they belonged to any other ethnic collectivity than the local community. Thus, in 1934–35 an investigation of the inhabitants of the marshy Pripet area (which between the two World Wars was included within Poland) showed that nearly half of those peasants who were ethnically White Ruthenians did not know that such a nationality existed and considered themselves as belonging to local communities.

Nevertheless, due to the initiative of intellectuals, social solidarity based on a common national culture has been continually, though slowly, spreading among the masses, first in cities, then in rural areas. Two methods have been used: *propaganda* and *education*. Nationalistic propaganda began much earlier than education, since it could be carried on orally by authoritative leaders indoctrinating the illiterate masses, whereas nationalistic education required first teaching the young generation a minimum of literary national culture. Moreover, long before national cultures emerged, the method of oral propaganda had been developed by the priests who spread and strengthened religious solidarity among the masses without teaching them to read the sacred books. Of course, after the masses learned to read, printed nationalistic propaganda could supplement the oral propaganda, but its essential content remained almost unchanged.

We find that the main techniques by which propagandists try to make the masses conscious of belonging to a united nationality are similar to those which served for many centuries to promote the solidarity of other social groups. The most effective of them are: the cult of heroes, myths of common descent and racial unity, attachment to the native land as a collective group possession, and appeal for united defense against a common enemy.

The cult of heroes

The cult of heroes is found in most societies and has been investigated by historians, ethnologists, and sociologists.[1] A hero impersonates the most important common values of a social group, and his continuous glorification contributes to the maintenance of group solidarity. While some heroes are purely mythical and indistinguishable from gods, the majority of them were real persons, though obviously idealized by their followers. An individual may become a hero during his life and remain a hero after his death, as long as the group continues to worship him. Often, however, his cult develops fully only after his death, since it is easier to idealize a dead person than a living one.

At the time when modern national cultures began to emerge, there were three types of heroes: (1) legendary folk heroes, who were not objects of cult, but became famous figures in story or poetry; (2) religious heroes—saints—whose regular cult was organized by the Church; (3) great kings and warriors, whose cult was initiated by political groups. Gradually many of these saints, kings, and warriors became *national* heroes, the common heroes of ethnic collectivities. Eventually, also, a new type of purely cultural hero as creative genius emerged.

Take some typical examples.

Quite a few saints were exalted as national heroes with the approval, sometimes on the initiative of the Church, Roman Catholic as well as Greek Orthodox, since the Church stimulated the active participation and solidarity of the faithful by adapting some of its ideas and practices to folk cultures. Thus, St. Martin, St. Denis, Ste. Geneviève were recognized as distinctly French. St. Stanislaw, who lived in the twelfth century, gradually became a Polish national saint, and his yearly cult persisted throughout Poland even in the twentieth century. St. John Nepomuk was made by the Catholic Church a national hero of Bohemia, to counteract the influence of Hussitism. The

1. Cf. Stefan Czarnowski, *Le Culte des héros . . .* (Paris, 1917); Gottfried Salomon, "Hero Worship," *Encyclopedia of the Social Sciences;* Sidney Hook, *The Hero in History* (New York: Day, 1942); Eric Russell Bentley, *A Century of Hero Worship* (Philadelphia: Lippincott, 1944); Dixon Wecter, *The Hero in America* (New York: Scribner, 1941).

83

2. Cf. Czarnowski, op. cit.

most significant instance of a saint who became the greatest and for centuries remained the only hero of a national society was St. Patrick of Ireland.[2] On the other hand, with the emergence of Protestantism, some prophets of the new religions were accepted by their followers as national heroes: John Huss as a Czech hero, Luther as a German hero.

The heroization of kings is very old, since kings were originally sacred, even divine. During the Middle Ages, a few kings became national heroes to the militant nobility—typically, Charlemagne as a French hero—but they do not seem to have been accepted as such by the masses. Some kings, however, became exalted as historical or legendary creators of order and protectors of the people. A few of them were canonized and also became religious heroes—St. Stephen of Hungary, St. Louis of France. Others remained secular—Frederick Barbarossa, Casimir the Great of Poland, Gedymin of Lithuania. The later heroization of the tsars of Russia as "Fathers of the Russian People" was purposely initiated and spread by political and religious leaders.

As national cultures developed, some kings became explicitly glorified by propagandists, not only as political heroes, but as supreme representatives of all the important values of the nationality over which they ruled: for instance, Louis XIV, the "Roi-Soleil," the ideal Frenchman. Napoleon was exalted (especially after his death), first, as heroic defender of the French Republic against foreign enemies; then as the Emperor, not of France, but of Frenchmen (Empereur des Français), who introduced order into the chaos following the Revolution; finally, as a martyr, the victim of foreign enemies and traitors.

Defenders of their own people against foreign invaders were often made national heroes. Some of them also became exalted as martyrs—Tsar Lazar of Serbia and Jeanne d'Arc, whose glorification appealed to the masses because she was of peasant origin. William Tell and Arnold von Winkelried became heroes in Swiss folklore. It was not easy to find German heroes who

84

functioned as defenders; in the sixteenth century Ulrich von Hutten tried to spread the cult of Hermann (Arminius) as the defender of Germans against Roman invaders, but his attempt was unsuccessful, and not until the second quarter of this century did Hermann gain recognition as the earliest German hero. During the nineteenth century quite a few such defenders of the distant or the recent past became heroized, e.g., Alexander Nevsky as defender of the Russian people against German and Swedish invaders, Minin and Pozarsky as Russian defenders against Polish invaders, Kosciuszko as defender of the Poles against the Russians. The heroization and public cult, not only of prominent leaders but of less important warriors who died in defense of their "nation," whether in the political or the cultural sense, has spread widely in recent times. (Cf. the cult of the Unknown Soldier.)

A well-known type of hero is the successful liberator of his people from oppression. The Russians have exalted Ivan the Great, who freed Russia from Tartar domination. A few more recent examples of liberating heroes are George Washington, Simon Bolivar, Garibaldi, Pilsudski, Masaryk, Gandhi.

The heroization of creative leaders in various realms of culture has been rather slow to develop—mainly because some general education is needed to have the masses of people appreciate their importance. However, nationalistic groups have found ways of making the masses of the people identify them and recognize their greatness, even without understanding their contributions. They follow the example of religious and political groups, erecting statues of the heroes, arranging public celebrations in their honor, and, if possible, pilgrimages to the places where they lived and acted or to their tombs. This is, for instance, how Dante, Michelangelo, Raphael, and—under Mussolini—even Virgil became Italian cultural heroes; Shakespeare, an English hero; Goethe and Wagner, German heroes; Copernicus, Mickiewicz, and Chopin, Polish heroes. Jefferson and Lincoln are now not only political, but cultural, heroes.

In recent times we notice an unprecedented, rapid growth of the cult of living national heroes, partly spontaneous, but mostly planfully developed by groups of their followers and spread by all kinds of propaganda and public ceremonies. These heroes combine all the heroic characteristics: like political heroes, they are makers of order; like military heroes, they are successful defenders and liberators; like religious saints, they are unimpeachably right; and like cultural heroes, they are great leaders in the growth of national culture. Mussolini, Hitler, and especially Stalin are the most conspicuous examples. Their history indicates how powerful and wide-spread the social solidarity can be which is due to the collective worship of supreme living heroes.

The myth of common descent and racial unity

Belief in common descent has always been a strong bond of solidarity. Rooted in kinship relations, it unified nonliterate clans and tribes, a Greek *fratria,* a Roman gens, a Chinese perpetual family, a European noble family. It often implies the conception that all descendants of common ancestors share the same blood or some half-mystical essence. The essence may be transmitted only by mothers or only by fathers or by both in different degrees. And this belief is usually accompanied by the assumption that all descendants of the same ancestors are biologically and psychologically alike, whatever their individual variations, and different from descendants of other ancestors. This assumption is the original basis of the doctrine of race, which developed first in tribal societies. Similarities within a tribe and differences between tribes, especially in bodily appearance, but also—or even primarily—in the conduct of members were considered inherited from tribal ancestors.

Needless to say, this doctrine was usually little more than a myth. And yet it became extended to large, long-lasting religious groups and recently even to national culture societies, although it is obviously impossible for all members of such a group to trace their origin directly to common ancestors or to prove that they constitute a distinct race, hereditarily alike and different from members of all other groups. The only possible proof of common descent would be indirect, based on historical evidence that the group has always been endogamous; and the only possible proof of racial unity would be if anthropological analysis of somatic traits of its members, in comparison with somatic traits of members of other groups, indubitably showed hereditary similarities and differences. Whereas, as a matter of fact, when historical and anthropological evidence is available, it usually disproves both assumptions. Nevertheless, belief in the truth of this doctrine can persist indefinitely. In this respect, it is like other kinds of myths which believers accept without regard to factual evidence.[3]

A good example of the persistence of this myth in a religious group is the belief of many Jews—i.e., of the people who share the Mosaic religion—that they are descendants of the same Biblical ancestors. This belief has been for eighteen centuries a powerful bond of social solidarity, since the "people of Israel" were defined in the Torah as the "chosen people" with a divine mission. It persists nowadays, in spite of the fact that in the light of somatic anthropology the hereditary traits of contemporary Jews differ more than those of any other modern collectivity (except perhaps the Chinese) which accepts the myth of common descent, and that some of these differences can be historically explained by partial religious integration and partial miscegenation of Israelites with groups of different backgrounds (e.g., with the Khazars, who accepted the Mosaic religion in the eighth century and many of whom migrated later to western Russia and Poland). And it is unfortunate that this assumption coincides with the popular doctrine of anti-Semites, that all the peoples who share or whose near ancestors shared the Mosaic religion are of the same race, with common and dis-

3. For a historico-critical survey of racial doctrines as applied to cultural collectivities, see, e.g., Frank H. Hankins, *The Racial Basis of Civilization* (New York: Knopf, 1924); Théophile Simar, *Etude critique sur la formation de la doctrine des races . . .* (Brussels, 1922); Louis L. Snyder, *Race* (New York: Longmans, 1939); Jacques Barzun, *Race: A Study of Modern Superstition* (New York: Harcourt, 1937); Franz Boas, *Race, Language and Culture* (New York: Macmillan, 1940); M. M. Ashley-Montagu, *Man's Most Dangerous Myth* (New York: Columbia University Press, 1945).

4. See, e.g., Hans E. K. Günter, *Rassenkunde des jüdischen Volkes* (Munich, 1930).

5. This is surprising in view of the fact that such application was discredited long ago: see, e.g., W. D. Babington, *Fallacies of Race Theories as Applied to National Characteristics* (London, 1895).

tinctive hereditary characteristics, psychological as well as biological.[4]

When we survey modern literature about nationalities, we discover that many authors treat a cultural nationality as almost coextensive with a race, implicitly or explicitly assuming that a distinct culture must be the product of a distinct race. For instance, quite a few books published in the United States apply, at least occasionally, the term "race" to Germans, Italians, Poles, Russians, Hungarians, Finns, Turks, Mexicans, Irishmen, etc.[5] Such an indiscriminate application of this term is even more general in popular speech. Apparently, those who use it are unaware that the identification of race with nationality was initiated by nationalistic ideologists who used the term "race" with evaluative connotations, postulating the inequality of races and claiming that the people who belonged to their own nationality were racially superior to people of other nationalities.

This claim has proved an effective instrument of nationalistic propaganda; for, by persuading the masses that they were hereditarily superior to peoples with different cultures, their solidarity in relation to those "racially inferior" foreigners was stimulated. To be sure, certain obstacles interfered with this solidarity—extreme clannishness, regional separatism, class divisions, historical evidence of racial mixtures. The racial myth alone was not always sufficient to overcome these obstacles, but it was certainly helpful.

Clannishness, in the sense of the exclusive inner solidarity of groups, each of which claimed a different ancestry, was for a long time a well-known obstacle in the way of Scottish national solidarity. Several other factors contributed to the final elimination of this obstacle—struggle against common enemies, cult of heroes, and creative growth of Scottish culture; but we should not ignore the contribution made by the myth of Scottish racial unity and superiority.

88

In recent times the most significant instance of the use of the racial myth to overcome clannishness was the ideology promulgated by Sun Yat-sen.[6] Belief in common ancestors and their cult had been for centuries the strongest and most lasting unifying force in China; but the largest social group united by this belief was the patrilineal clan with a common name, and there were more than 150 such clans without any social bond between them. Sun Yat-sen hoped to overcome this separatism by persuading the masses of Chinese people that all these clans were integral parts of one race, with common origin rooted in a distant past. He did not explicitly claim at first that the Chinese race was superior, only that it was equal to other races; however, his idea of the moral superiority of Chinese culture as the original product of Chinese people could be interpreted as a proof of racial superiority.

How influential the myth of racial unity and superiority can be in overcoming regional separatism is well exemplified by the growing prestige and the wide acceptance of the national name *deutsch* as applicable to inhabitants of many regions with considerable differences in tradition and culture. One of the early nationalistic writers, Wieland, at the end of the eighteenth century, stated that in the locality where he was brought up one of the most contemptuous names by which a boy could be called by his companions, almost as bad as *Esel* (ass), was *deutscher Michel*. Whereas a hundred years later, although a Bavarian or a Saxon still considered himself superior to a Prussian and vice versa, most of them were proud of being *deutsch,* since this name was consistently used by propagandists to denote a type of person inherently more valuable than foreigners, who were unworthy of this name. And we know how this pride increased under the impact of the Nazi myth of a racially supreme *deutsches Herrenvolk.* Not so effective was the myth of a superior Anglo-Saxon race which some ideologists attempted to spread not only in England, but throughout the

6. Cf. Sun Yat-sen, *San Min Chu I, The Three Principles of the People* (Shanghai, 1927); Paul M. Lineberger, *The Political Doctrine of Sun Yat-Sen* (Baltimore: Johns Hopkins, 1937).

United States, to insure the solidarity of the descendants of the people who had created English culture and to promote their domination over all "racially inferior" nationalities.

The myth of racial unity encountered considerable opposition from the hereditary upper classes, wherever the old myth still survived that they were racially different from the lower classes, as in France, where Gobineau tried to prove that the French nobles were superior to the masses, because they were descendants of the Franks, of pure or nearly pure "Aryan" ("Nordic") race.[7] Nevertheless, the new myth proved more influential than the old. Russian nationalists—some Slavophiles and later populists (*narodniki*)—emphasized that the peasants were the bearers of the most valuable Russian hereditary traits; although they were themselves nobles, they considered the Russian nobility as belonging to the same race as the peasants and treated its cultural differentiation from the masses as a symptom of decadence. Another solution of the hereditary class problem, much more satisfactory to the nobility, was offered by ideologists who, while accepting the doctrine of common descent and racial unity of all classes, claimed that the upper class included the most typical representatives of their race, possessing in the highest degree all its valuable traits. This claim was supported by some social Darwinists who considered class stratification a result of natural selection: "the fittest" rose to the top, and their descendants remained there so long as they inherited the fitness of their ancestors.[8]

Historical evidence of the mixture of races need not interfere with the myth of racial unity, especially when that mixture occurred in a distant past; but, in any case, mass propaganda does not have to take into consideration reliable historical knowledge. If the races which have mixed are considered to have been valuable, their blend is supposed to contain a combination of their best original characteristics. Thus, the French are presumed to have inherited in various degrees the best racial traits of their Gallic ancestors, the early Roman conquerors,

7. Arthur de Gobineau, *Essai sur l'inégalité des races humaines* (Paris, 1853-55).

8. See, e.g., Otto Ammon, *Die Gesellschaftsordnung und ihre natürlichen Grundlagen* (Jena, 1895).

and the later Teutonic invaders. But if one of the blended races is considered inferior, the mixture is simply ignored. Thus, German nationalists who regard Slavs as an inferior race ignore the historical evidence that Western Slavs were not exterminated after the German conquests, but Germanized and for centuries mixed with their conquerors, and that the "inferior" Prussians who were conquered by the Knights of the Cross in East Prussia did not simply disappear, but became Germanized. Recent miscegenation, however, cannot be ignored, even with an "inferior" race. We know that the Nazis excluded from the German nationality and branded as Jews anybody who had one grandparent of Jewish descent, and that many Southerners in the United States still refuse to recognize as a full participant in the American national society anybody who has had one Negro ancestor, however distant.

Whenever two nationalities have been involved in long-lasting conflicts and mutual prejudice has developed, mass appeal to social solidarity is certainly more effective, if accompanied by the claim that the other, hostile, nationality is racially inferior and that the negative prejudice against it is justified. For instance, in contrast with those Russian nationalists who proclaimed that the Russians were superior to all other Slavs and consequently destined to lead or even absorb them, some Polish nationalists insisted that the Russians (called "Moskale," as distinct from Ukrainians and White Ruthenians) are hereditarily inferior to Poles and other Slavic peoples, for they are not really Slavs, but a mixture of races with predominantly Mongolian traits, mostly inherited from their Tartar conquerors. We remember how the German claim to racial superiority was countered during World War I by the popular assertion that the Germans are descendants of the "Huns," and during World War II by the doctrine that they are a psychologically degenerate race. A similar counterclaim was made against the "Japs."

The popularization of racial myths is made easier if accompanied by concrete verbal descriptions or pictorial representations of allegedly typical persons of "our own" superior race and of the inferior foreign races. These methods have been widely used in recent times, especially with the development of modern mass media of communication; but their origin can be traced back to folk cultures. In folk tales the heroes represent ideal types of the people who perpetuate the tales, whereas typical "foreigners" are usually the very antithesis of these heroes. They are not always evil or dangerous, as the white "foreign devils" were in some areas of China; often they are merely ridiculous. It is interesting, for instance, that in several Slavic languages the old name for Germans originally meant the "mute ones," those who cannot speak; and in western Polish dialects cockroaches are still called "Prussians." We are familiar with the contemptuous names by which foreign immigrants of various nationalities have been called in American slang. In nearly every language there are popular proverbs ascribing to foreigners undesirable traits and often advising what to do or not to do in dealing with them, though the foreigners may be inhabitants of a neighboring region, not very different culturally from "our people."

Visual representations of perfect native figures and caricatures of foreigners are also found in the folk art of many traditional cultures. Later, some men of letters and professional artists continued to create idealized types of people of their own nationality and antithetic types of foreigners. Thus, when positive and especially negative racial myths began to be planfully popularized by nationalistic propagandists, considerable material was already at hand from which such stereotypes could be easily produced.

We notice, however, that the influence of racial myths is decreasing. They have been explicitly rejected by communist ideologists, ignored by the League of Nations and by the United Nations. The absurdity of the racial mythology promulgated by the Nazi regime and its destructive consequences discredited

more than any scientific criticism the doctrine that nationalities
are coextensive with races.

National land as common and exclusive group possession

Possessive claims of social groups to the total land inhabited
by their members are very old. These claims are not merely
economic, but moral and often religious; they are superimposed
upon whatever rights of economic ownership to portions of this
land may be granted to smaller groups or individual members.

Thus, in most tribal societies the land on which members
of the tribe had lived—whether they were hunters, pastoral
nomads, or agriculturalists—was an exclusive possession of the
tribe and endowed with some degree of sacredness. It often had
a holy center where deities or mythical ancestors abided. Its
borders were protected by magical powers or divine beings;
a foreigner who crossed such a border without special permis-
sion and personal purification profaned the sacredness of the
land and incurred the danger of death at the hand of the
protective deities or the tribesmen. When the role of sacred
king began to evolve, the whole territory of his kingdom, as
well as all the people, was under his magico-religious protection, and foreigners could not enter without gaining his per-
mission. If foreign warriors actually did invade it by force after
having been made immune from magico-religious dangers by
enemy magicians or priests, the king had to defend it by combining his mystical power with military power; he either ap-
pointed and consecrated a war leader or acted himself in that
capacity. An ancient city-state had a holy center; its urban area
was sacred, surrounded and protected physically and magically
by walls; the rural area around it had less sacredness, but still
its border was entrusted to the protection of minor magico-
religious forces.

Such groups were united not merely by common material interests, but by common ideational culture. It was their social unity and the separatism based on their common culture which made them claim exclusive possession of the land which they inhabited and limited permanently the right to inhabit this land to people who shared their culture; this included, of course, their descendants, to whom their culture would be transmitted. Originally this culture was traditional, based on face-to-face contacts; consequently, their numbers and the size of their territory were quite limited.

When the early kingdoms and later some city-states expanded by conquest, the conquering groups superimposed their possessive claims to the land they conquered and controlled upon the claims of the original inhabitants. This obviously resulted in social conflicts, which could be partly solved by compromise, when conquerors granted provincial autonomy to the conquered, but disappeared only if in the course of time the conquerors and the conquered became culturally integrated. Eventually, as we know, territorial unity and territorial separatism came to be based primarily upon political and military rule. The state, with an authoritarian government and practical monopoly of force, assumed supreme possession and guardianship of the territory inhabited by its subjects. The social name of the state and the geographical name of its territory usually became identical. Sometimes the state was named from its territory, e.g., the Netherlands, Italy, Argentina, recently India; sometimes the territory and the state from the ethnic name of the people who occupied most of the territory, e.g., Scotland (land of the Scots), Poland (land of the Poles), Finland (land of the Finns). Frequently the ethnic name of the conquering group which built the state was applied to the state *and* to its entire territory, even though the majority of its original inhabitants formed several ethnically diverse groups. Roman war lords and political rulers applied their title as citizens of Rome to the empire they ruled and to the whole territory controlled by this

94

empire, however different culturally from the Romans the inhabitants of its many areas were. The word "France" was first introduced to cover that part of Gaul which was conquered and ruled by the Frankish kings. "Anglia," eventually "England," denoted at first the land conquered and the state organized by a relatively small group of invaders. The land conquered by Ottoman Turks was given their name, though the vast majority of its inhabitants were not and never became Turks. Russia under the Tsarist regime denoted the Tsarist Empire and the entire territory conquered and ruled by the "Russians," including more than a hundred non-Russian ethnic groups, since that part of the territory which the Russians ("Great Russians") inhabited was considered the most valuable, almost sacred. This name is still used by Western writers, although the communists have substituted for it the name "Union of Soviet Socialist Republics."

How did these names for large territories become accepted as symbols of national unity by masses of people, many of whom never moved beyond the limits of a local community or at most a provincial area, knowing little, if anything, about the territory as a whole?[9] How did they come to believe that these territories constituted their common possession, supremely valuable to all of them? Whence the popularity and the sentimentality of the well-known national songs expressing this belief? Consider, for instance, the French national anthem "La Marseillaise," sung after the Revolution by soldiers from Marseilles and beginning "Allons, enfants de la patrie. Le jour de gloire est arrivé"; "patrie" evidently meant France, not merely Marseilles to these soldiers. The Polish national song, started by legionnaires serving under Bonaparte in Italy ("Poland has not yet perished, so long as we are alive"), expresses the certainty that all Polish land taken by enemies will be recovered and the Polish state rebuilt. We are familiar with the American songs: "My country, 'tis of thee" and "America the beautiful." Perhaps the most emphatic expression of this attachment

9. The problem is treated, though not very thoroughly, by Robert Michels in his *Patriotismus*.

to the national land and its high valuation is the famous German song "Deutschland, Deutschland über alles, über alles in der Welt."

In surveying the origin of this conception of "national land" and its spread through propaganda, we see that it is rooted first in the old idea of "patria" or "fatherland," and obviously connected with the myth of common origin. "Our land" is "the land of our fathers and forefathers," the land where they lived and where "we" were born. Our ancestors made it valuable; it contains the agglomerated products of successive generations—cultivated fields, gardens, homes, temples, public buildings, etc.—to which all of us, their descendants, have possessive rights, prior to those of any outsiders. Moreover, this is the land where our ancestors are buried; their graves make it sacred.

While this idea is easily accepted or even spontaneously developed by inhabitants of an old village community or an old city with its surrounding rural area, it can also be and indeed has been extended to all the areas whose inhabitants are supposed to share the same cultural heritage derived from common ancestors, however distant in time. Cult of common heroes strengthens the idea, and it acquires a practical significance for the masses of people whenever interdependence between the various areas of the total country increases. There is religious interdependence when centers of pilgrimage, temples, and priestly groups are scattered over the country, and every area can provide religious leaders functioning on behalf of other areas. This was the main foundation for the concept of India as the common land of all Hindu people.[10] Political interdependence is manifest if and insofar as representatives of various areas participate in the common government. Economic interdependence becomes obvious when industry and transportation expand. Finally, interdependence may grow between the local and the regional centers of national culture. Thus, "our land," "the land of our ancestors" becomes for the masses

10. Cf. Radhakumud Mookerji, *The Fundamental Unity of India* (London, 1941): "The primary factor of a Nationality is the possession of a common country; a common fatherland is preliminary to all national development. The formation of an Indian nation must wait on the realization by the Indians of the whole of India as their common mother country claiming their loyalty and service" (p. xv). According to the author, the extension of the geographic horizon of Hindu thinkers and leaders has been growing since the Vedic age.

96

of people the spatial receptacle of most, if not all, of their important values.

The need of defense against foreign enemies

According to some social thinkers, this is the universal and the only efficient factor of social solidarity; for within every social group exist conflicts which can be overcome only if the group is involved in a struggle against another group; if there is no such struggle, the group becomes disintegrated.[11] What these thinkers do not take into consideration is that no inter-group struggle exists without in-group solidarity. This applies to intertribal struggles, interfamily vendettas, interstate wars, conflicts between religious groups. There can be no doubt, however, that the solidarity of a group is strengthened when another group threatens to harm its members, to appropriate or destroy its common values, to endanger its very existence. The group tends to unite in defense against such an aggressive enemy. The idea that the enemy is the aggressor, while "we" are the defenders, always has more popular appeal and influence than the opposite idea. As we noticed above, defending heroes are much more numerous than aggressive heroes.

There are apparent exceptions. Religious societies, with the mission of converting all mankind to their "true" faith; imperialistic states, with the mission of creating an orderly, peaceful world empire; nationalistic societies, with the mission of imposing their supreme culture upon inferior peoples; lately communist societies, with the mission of introducing the only "right" kind of social order into all human societies: these are not expected to be merely on the defensive. Aggression is essential for the fulfillment of their missions; and, according to their own ideologies, it is justifiable, since their ultimate purpose is altruistic.

However, these missions are usually undertaken by fully

11. E.g., Gustav Ratzenhofer, *Wesen und Zwech der Politik* (Leipzig, 1893).

97

indoctrinated and well-organized ruling groups; the masses of people belonging to their societies seem to manifest very little active interest in these missions. Consequently, to gain the support of the masses, leaders frequently appeal to the need for common defense against actual or potential aggressors, bearers of "evil," dangerous enemies of the "good." Such appeals have been widely used in religious struggles—e.g., between Christians and Moslems, Catholics and Protestants— no matter which group actually started the struggle. The attempt of Hitler, his sponsors, and followers to fulfill the German world mission began with an appeal to German solidarity in defense against dangerous enemies. The most dangerous of these were the Jews, for they undermined German unity and profaned German purity from the inside and allied themselves with outside enemies: capitalistic Western powers and communist Russia. During the last few years communist propagandists have been trying to strengthen the solidarity of the masses within the Soviet Union and in its satellite countries by emphasizing the need for common defense against outside capitalistic aggressors, especially American "warmongers," and against inside traitors and "enemies of the people."

Of course, the appeal to defensive solidarity is effective in unifying the masses of people who presumably share the same national culture, if the enemies are obviously cultural foreigners and really act as aggressors to the detriment of "our people." Thus the danger of military invasion usually promotes social solidarity among the inhabitants of all the regions threatened by this invasion and helps overcome, at least temporarily, inner class struggles and political conflicts. Napoleon's invasions undoubtedly increased German, Spanish, and Russian national solidarity. We know how influential the Japanese invasion was in stimulating Chinese national unity; even the struggle between the Kuomintang and the communists subsided for a time and did not revive until after the Japanese defeat. Even more significant was the consequence of the destructive German invasion into the Soviet Union: the rebellious nationalistic trends of Ukrainians, White Ruthenians, Poles, and Lithuanians against Russian domination and the general latent rebellion against the communist regime gave way for a time to common solidarity in defense against the invaders.

The ideal of national independence from foreign domination becomes accepted by the masses if and insofar as it is possible to persuade the "common people" that the ruling nationality is their enemy, that its rule is oppressive and injurious to them, and that they should unite in defense against their oppressors. The privileged status of members of the dominant nationality, all manifestations of racial prejudice, economic exploitation, use of violent methods of coercion, limitation of the rights of subject peoples, the tightening of political controls: all help to make this appeal effective. This is how, for instance, the mass solidarity of subject nationalities in Tsarist Russia and in Prussia increased during the second half of the nineteenth century.

In the appeal of Indian nationalists for the solidarity of Indian peoples, the need for common defense against British imperialism, presumably harmful to the masses of Indians, was continually emphasized.[12] Sun Yat-sen's appeal to Chinese solidarity also included the need for defense against political and economic penetration of China by the Western powers.

12. It was still being over-emphasized ten years ago by Nehru, *The Unity of India* (London, 1941).

This defensive solidarity is most obvious, however, when found in groups subjected to persecution on the part of a powerful hostile group. It is then particularly significant because defensive cooperation is dangerous for all individuals who participate in it, and this means that the group must be recognized as supremely valuable to its members. Religious groups furnish many examples: early Christian groups persecuted by certain Roman rulers, heretical groups subjected to the persecution of the dominant church, and especially Jewish groups, whose faith and unity were preserved under persecution throughout centuries. Heroization of the victims as martyrs undoubtedly contributed greatly to the solidarity of these groups.

Defensive solidarity on the part of national culture societies was clearly manifested in recent times by their underground resistance to persecution after the Nazi invasion. Since the war, a considerable amount of material has been published concerning French, Dutch, Belgian, Norwegian, Polish, Czech, Serbian, and Greek resistance. In the light of this material, it is clear that the effectiveness of resistance depended partly on the methods used by the invader, partly on the previous training of the invaded nationality in collective rebellion. The Nazis granted cultural freedom and some degree of political autonomy to the French and the Norwegians, on the condition that they submit to puppet regimes, but none to the Poles, the Czechs, or the Serbs. The resistance of the latter nationalities was consequently more solidary. Moreover, the Poles and the Serbs had a century-old training in violent revolt against foreign domination; their underground was therefore the most active and best organized.

The development of public education in national culture

However influential oral propaganda might be in stimulating ethnic solidarity, its effectiveness in the long run was obviously limited by the fact that the illiterate masses could not learn much about any literary culture or appreciate its significance as a bond of social unity. Already in the eighteenth century some nationalistic thinkers decided that regular education of the entire younger generation in their national culture, accompanied by persistent inculcation of loyalty to the society sharing this culture, would be the best method for making the masses of people solidary. This would require, first, a wide use of printing for the purpose of making the main

100

components of the national culture accessible (at least in simplified form) to the entire young generation; second, the organization of numerous schools to help the young of all classes understand their culture and to prepare them for active participation in their society.

Many obstacles, however, impeded this development. In the first place, the spread of literary education in general was obstructed by the class hierarchy. According to the higher classes, lower classes did not need any such education; they were supposed to follow the guidance of their superiors. Nor did the lower classes generally believe that they or their children needed it, except when education helped an individual rise in social status, as when a peasant boy was given the opportunity to become a minister of religion. As late as the end of the nineteenth century, many European peasants and even American farmers in some areas considered school education a waste of time, unless a boy was meant to be trained for some urban occupation or profession.

Furthermore, since schools had to be supported, the well-to-do people who contributed most to their support expected them to serve their own interests. Thus, in England the schools supported by upper-class parents were reserved for upper-class children. Church schools, when the Church obtained its funds from well-to-do believers, also often limited their pupils to upper-class children, e.g., convent schools for girls.[13] Even in colleges preparing ministers of religion, the majority of students came from the well-to-do classes, although promising young men from lower classes were sometimes admitted and educated at the cost of the Church. Schools supported by a state seldom admitted students of low-class origin. Thus, military and naval schools, in France under the monarchies, in England, in Prussia, in Austria, and in Russia, trained professional officers recruited almost exclusively from the higher classes. So did the schools—especially the law schools—preparing students for important bureaucratic roles. And schools

13. A typical example was convent education for girls in France at the beginning of the eighteenth century; cf. Mme Françoise d'Aubigné de Maintenon, *Conseils et instructions aux demoiselles pour leur conduite dans le monde*, 2 vols. (Paris, 1851). Convents of the Sacré Coeur order maintained schools for upper-class girls in most European countries throughout the nineteenth century.

101

supported by capitalists originally prepared selected individuals of the capitalist class for leading economic roles.

Under these conditions, education in the national language was not necessarily connected with inculcation of national loyalty. In schools supported by the hereditary nobility, class loyalty was explicitly or implicitly imparted to the students. The churches exalted religious loyalties above all others. The state demanded that officers and bureaucrats be trained to serve loyally the government then in power. In schools controlled by capitalists, the economic and political solidarity of the upper bourgeoisie was emphasized.

This does not imply, however, that these different loyalties always conflicted with national loyalty. They did not conflict in England, where the influential gentry, the clergy, and the bourgeoisie were, from the eighteenth century, strongly for English cultural unity; nor in France, where by the end of the seventeenth century French culture was considered by the royal government, the nobility, and the bourgeoisie to be an important factor in the unity and prestige of the Kingdom of France.[14] In Poland before the partitions, among the nobility who ruled the nation and the bourgeoisie who were Polonized, and even in the Church, nationality conscious leaders took the upper hand when the danger from Russia, Austria, and Prussia became imminent. Education in Polish culture and loyalty to the Polish state came to be recognized as supremely important, and a Ministry of Education—the first in history—was organized.

The conditions were different in Italy and Germany. There kings and princes—in Italy also the Pope—resisted attempts to educate the young generation in national loyalty, since every collective tendency toward unification would interfere with their sovereignty. Moreover, in Germany the division between Protestants and Catholics sometimes prevented education from promoting the general national solidarity of the German people. As late as the last quarter of the nineteenth century, the

14. Cf. Carlton J. Hayes, *The Historical Evolution of Modern Nationalism* and *France, a Nation of Patriots.*

102

so-called "Kulturkampf" under the leadership of Bismarck attempted to eliminate entirely from Prussia the ideological influence of the Roman Catholic Church.

But, whatever the relationship between the various loyalties
which schools were trying to impart to the young generation,
universal education of lower classes did not begin until the
democratic ideal promulgated by nationalistic thinkers and
leaders became accepted and was applied by influential organized groups.

According to this ideal, if all citizens were to participate
actively in government, they had to be prepared for this participation. And in order to overcome the personal inequality
between the illiterate masses and the well-educated, higher-
class elite which monopolized almost completely the important
social roles—officers, bureaucrats, diplomats, clergymen, doc-
tors, lawyers, scientists, university professors, bankers, industrial managers, etc.—a minimum of education had to be accessible to all, and everybody ought to have the opportunity
to rise from a lower to a higher educational level. Only education in the national literary culture could fulfill these requirements; both on the lower level, where it was relatively easy
to learn a literary language for people who already spoke dialectical variants of this language, and on higher levels, where all
professional roles except those of clergymen were based on the
secular culture.

The first attempt to introduce universal school education
in any national language and culture was started in France by
the Jacobins and continued later, though with some interrup-
tions, under different governments until it was fully achieved
under the Third Republic. Next it began in the United States
after the Revolution, somewhat later in those European countries where the democratic ideal was gaining influence. When
this ideal began to penetrate into countries ruled by autocratic
governments, the latter undertook to educate the masses in such
a way as to counteract the spread of democracy. Thus, in Aus-

tria and in Prussia the task of developing popular school education was assumed by the governments, but the schools were subjected to rigid governmental control, and the teachers were forced to indoctrinate the young in complete loyalty to the monarchical regimes. A similar, though slower, development of popular education occurred during the second half of the nineteenth century in Russia. As we know, soon after the overthrow of these monarchies, German national education came to be completely dominated by the Nazi regime, planfully indoctrinating the entire young generation in absolute loyalty to the Führer and the government which supported him; while in the Soviet Union and lately in the satellite countries, organized education in the national language and culture, on all levels, is accompanied by an exceptionally efficient inculcation of unconditional loyalty to the communist regime.

In countries dominated by foreign powers, the effort to spread education in the national culture and national loyalty is, of course, particularly difficult. A good example of this was furnished by Poland under Prussia and Russia in the last quarter of the nineteenth century and at the beginning of the twentieth. At that time, all schools were subjected to governmental control. The use of Polish was forbidden. Under German domination German was the language of instruction in all subjects except religion. Likewise, under Russian domination, the language of instruction was Russian, though a short, nonobligatory course was given in Polish, as one of the "foreign" languages. Then the function of transmitting Polish national culture was assumed by innumerable private groups. Of course, parents who had been educated in Polish taught it to their children. In cities, private teachers of Polish gave lessons; many intellectuals who performed other roles also acted as teachers of small groups; and students who had learned Polish from their elders taught it to younger students. In rural areas wives and daughters of estate-owners held classes for workers and peasants. And in both urban and rural areas many priests, when teaching religion, also taught Polish reading and writing.

The most interesting result of all this, however, was the development of self-education. In many villages, peasants who with some help had learned to read and write Polish continued their self-education by reading periodicals and books, transmitted their self-acquired learning to organized groups of neighbors or their children, and stimulated these to further self-education.[15] On a higher level, in nearly every class of every secondary school secret self-educational groups were organized for collective study of Polish history and literature. Eventually, most of these groups undertook the task of cooperative self-education in other realms of knowledge which were not being taught in schools—political science, economics, philosophy, psychology, sociology, etc.—in preparation for future intellectual leadership.[16] The effectiveness of this private, informal national education and self-education was manifested after Poland regained independence. Although only in Galicia (that part of Poland which had autonomy within the Austrian Empire) were Polish public schools permitted, after only ten years or so a public school system was functioning fully throughout Poland with properly trained teachers.[17]

General programs of popular education in national culture and loyalty

Wherever popular school education has developed, its basic programs are quite uniform. This was originally due to the initiative of the educational thinkers and leaders who shared national ideologies. They postulated that the main function of schools is to prepare pupils for membership in their national society, planned teaching programs to include those subjects which they considered essential for this function, and eventually wrote textbooks in those subjects. The establishment of teachers' colleges and associations of teachers which accepted

15. A survey of this self-education was included in *The Polish Peasant,* W. I. Thomas and F. Znaniecki (Boston: Badger, 1918-20).

16. I participated in such an association for five years, and later (1921-38) collected considerable material about similar associations throughout Poland.

17. Other kinds of associations where young people learned national culture and loyalty were formed in some subjugated countries. For instance, such was the main function of the Czech Sokols, seemingly a purely sport association: Edward Spatny, "The Sokols" (manuscript).

these programs has resulted in a growing uniformity of general education in primary and secondary schools, whatever the differences in special subjects taught to pupils in preparation for specific occupational roles. Bureaucratic governmental groups often contribute to this uniformity by imposing their programs upon all public schools, typically in France, in Germany, and in Russia. In the United States, however, although the government of each state tends to uniformize the curricula of primary and secondary schools within its borders, the Federal government does nothing to promote such uniformity; nonetheless, education in American culture and loyalty is fundamentally alike all over the United States.

In comparing the educational programs of various national culture societies, we discern considerable differences in the evaluative conceptions of "foreign" nationalities and their cultures which are imparted to the young generation; but, as far as their own nationality is concerned, these programs are essentially similar.

Of course, reading and writing in the national language are the primary and basic subjects, and all other subjects are taught in this language. On lower educational levels no other language is taught, unless the ethnic group from which the children come is dependent politically or economically on another, and the use of both languages is necessary for full active participation in collective life. For instance, English is taught in schools maintained by immigrant groups in the United States and in urban French-Canadian schools. In the federated and autonomous republics of the Soviet Union, Russian is now being taught to children in addition to their national language, and it may soon become the dominant common language.

If the language is shared with some other nationality, a tendency often appears to emphasize dialectical differences and to stabilize certain innovations. Thus, Noah Webster included in his elementary textbooks for American children some components of the new dialects which were evolving in New Eng-

106

land.[18] Since his time the growing differences between the American language and the "King's English" have become generally recognized by schoolteachers.

Now the national language is usually explicitly or implicitly exalted, in contrast to the period when modern languages were considered inferior to the older classical languages. Children in France, Italy, Spain, Germany, England, Russia, and Poland are now being taught to appreciate their native language as the most valuable or at least as equally valuable as any other language. At first, this was sometimes difficult, because of the unequal prestige of modern national languages, especially from the point of view of the higher classes. Thus, in the second half of the eighteenth century and the first half of the nineteenth, French was generally considered by the nobility and the gentry in Central and Eastern Europe to be superior to their own national languages. At the beginning of the nineteenth century, Danish had a higher prestige in Norway than Norwegian.[19] It was not easy for Hindu national leaders to overcome the prestige which English acquired among the upper classes in India, since only Sanscrit could claim superiority, and Sanscrit was not a living national language. Even now, this matter of prestige is an important issue for some nationalities. We mentioned before (Chapter Two) the competition between Jewish national leaders who prefer Yiddish and those who favor Hebrew as the common language of the Jewish people. Although Yiddish as a secular literary language, originating in spoken dialects, was fully developed and used by the majority of Jews before the Nazi genocide, its prestige remained obviously lower than that of Hebrew as a sacred language. Consequently, attempts to develop a national secular language from Hebrew have multiplied and become increasingly successful, until by now in New Israel only this language is taught, while Yiddish is rejected altogether.

The prestige of any language is manifestly connected with the prestige of the literature written in this language; therefore,

18. Harry R. Warfel, *Noah Webster, Schoolmaster to America* (New York: Macmillan, 1936).

19. Not so a century later. Cf. David A. Anderson, *The School System of Norway* (Boston: Gorham Press, 1912).

national literature is taught and usually exalted wherever popular school education has developed, typically in France, England, Germany, Italy, and Poland. The greatness of Russian literature was emphasized in Russian schools during the Tsarist regime; this stopped for a while after the Bolshevik Revolution, since most of the Russian writers had been "bourgeois," but has been fully resumed during the last fifteen years. Foreign modern literatures may not be entirely ignored, but less attention is paid to them.

When a new national literature has recently evolved from an older literature, both are being taught. Thus, in the United States English literature of past historical periods is still an important subject, since it is considered a cultural heritage which American people share, but pupils are also taught to appreciate the modern developments of an original American literature. A similar appreciation of old Spanish or Portuguese literature, as well as of new contributions by authors of their own nationality, is found in Latin American countries.

Teaching history is, obviously, the most general and effective way of inculcating national loyalty. Usually much more time is devoted to the history of "our society" than to the history of all other societies, although sometimes ancient and medieval history are studied insofar as they presumably help to give understanding of the early period of "our history." The latter is both ethnic and political; the emphasis may be on one aspect or the other, depending on which is the more inclusive and glorious. Thus, German history as taught in schools is primarily the history of the German people and emphasizes the political history of the most important states which they formed in the course of centuries. English history centers around the history of England and the English people, but expands to include the history of other peoples who became parts of "Great Britain" and, finally, the history of the entire British Empire and its peoples. American history is primarily the political history of the United States, and only secondarily is it the ethnic history of the peoples who became included in it.

The national past is traced back as far as possible, and schoolteachers are frequently expected to introduce the conception of a superior common origin, however distant, if not of all participants in the national society, at least of those who presumably constitute its permanent and leading part. This conception is borrowed from those semi-mythical doctrines developed by nationalistic historians and propagandists (which we have discussed) and often presented in textbooks in a simplified, easily understandable form. It was highly emphasized in German textbooks under the Nazi regime, in Italian textbooks under the Fascist regime, and in prewar Japanese textbooks; but it was included also in French textbooks, in some Russian textbooks under the Tsarist regime, and recently in communist textbooks, which begin again to exalt the age-old greatness of the Russian people, although the idea of a hereditary racial superiority has been emphatically rejected.[20]

But even when the doctrine of common descent and the exaltation of the early history or prehistory of alleged national ancestors is not imparted to school pupils, the later history is almost universally idealized.[21] Biographies of national heroes impersonating supreme human values, but presented in such a way as to make them interesting to youngsters, are everywhere essential components of school education.[22] Perhaps the most striking example is the revival of heroic biographies in Russian schools, including those of autocratic tsars like Peter the Great and Ivan the Terrible. Exaltation of the national past is achieved by selecting and imparting to the young the knowledge of those historical events which added to national glory and of those activities in which "our nation" was essentially "right."[23] Anything that detracts from national glory, anything that appears wrong, if it cannot be omitted, is ascribed to the penetration of foreign influences and especially to the aggressive

20. The growing nationalism in Russian education can be ascertained by comparing the following works: René Fülop-Miller, *Geist und Gesicht des Bolschevismus* (Vienna: 1926); Samuel N. Harper, *Civic Training in Soviet Russia* (Chicago: University of Chicago Press, 1929); Albert Pinkevich, *The New Education in the Soviet Republic* (New York: Day, 1930); N. Hans and S. Hessen, *Educational Policy in Soviet Russia* (London, 1930); B. P. Yesipov and N. K. Goncharov, "I want to be like Stalin," *Pedagogika*, ed. George Counts (New York: Day, 1947). See also Nikolas Timasheff, *The Great Retreat* (New York: Dutton, 1940).

21. Ted Morgan, "National Literature and History in American Schools" (manuscript).

22. Seymour Corenson, "A Study of Hero Worship in American Schools" (manuscript).

23. Robert Liljander, "Cultural Nationalism in American Public Schools since World War I" (manuscript).

24. Two international confer-
ences on the teaching of history were devoted mainly to
this problem: June, 1932, at
the Hague; and June, 1934, at
Basle.

25. Argentina and Brazil later
reached such an agreement,
but their past conflicts were
much less important than those
between the Scandinavian nationalities.

tendencies of foreign enemies. Whenever wars or other conflicts occurred between two nationalities, the textbooks describing these conflicts for school pupils usually give different interpretations for each nationality; and according to these, their own nationality is always right and the other nationality always wrong. When attempts were made to eliminate such antithetic interpretations, because they imparted prejudices to the young,[24] only Sweden, Norway, and Denmark agreed to give school pupils impartial descriptions of their past conflicts.[25]

Geography, as taught in schools, is another subject which promotes national solidarity. The geography of "our land," or of "our country," is generally treated as more important than that of any other part of the globe. The frontiers of "our land" are frequently stretched as far as possible. If the territory of the state controlled by a nationality is wider than the land inhabited by the people of this nationality, all of it is included in school textbooks: thus, the Russian geography taught under the Tsarist regime included the entire territory of the empire in Europe and Asia, even though only a part of this territory was inhabited by Russians ("Great Russians"). If narrower, "our land" is made to include all the areas which now are at least in part inhabited or which formerly were inhabited by our own nationality, to whatever state they belong. Thus, Polish geography books during the period of partition included not only the territory of the former Kingdom of Poland, actually inhabited by Poles, but also in the east the territory of the former Grand-Duchy of Lithuania, on the ground that many of its inhabitants, though not originally Polish, had been Polonized; and in the west that part of Prussia which was originally inhabited by Poles, even though the majority of its present population were Germans. *Italia irredenta*—especially the southern Tyrol, Trieste, and Corsica—was included in books on Italian geography at the beginning of this century. After the Franco-Prussian War, both French and German geographical textbooks claimed Alsace-Lorraine; and after World

110

War I German geographies also included all of Silesia, the Polish province of Poznan ("Posen"), Eastern Pomerania ("West Prussia"), and Sudetenland. The conception of India as a geographic whole, the common land of all its inhabitants, is already being used in organized education as a foundation for the ideal of a united Indian society.

Besides language and literature, other specific components of national culture form parts of the program of public education. Patriotic songs and popular national music are taught in nearly all schools; children and adolescents learn about the most famous products of national art—architecture, painting, sculpture. Certain customs and mores are transmitted to the young as distinctive national traits; and conformity with them is interpreted as a proof of moral superiority over nationalities which do not conform with them. Political ideals and certain basic legal principles are taught in schools as superior products of "our own" nationality—typically in England, in the United States, in republican France, in imperial and later Nazi Germany, in Fascist Italy, and in present-day Russia. Finally, certain economic ideals are taught and exalted—"American individualism," the ideal of "free enterprise," and several national variants of collectivistic ideals, ranging from cooperation through democratic socialism to communism.

five

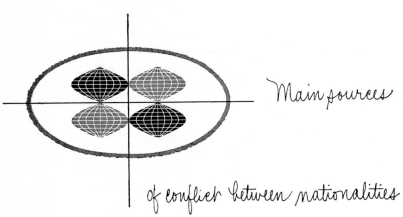

Main sources

of conflict between nationalities

Expansion of national culture societies

Students of nationalism have been primarily concerned with international conflicts, especially with those which result in political and military struggles. Inasmuch as there can be no conflict between social groups as such unless each group is (in some measure, at least) solidary, we had first of all to investigate the problem: How does a modern nationality become solidary, that is, socially united? We have already seen how strong this solidarity can become when a nationality is struggling for independence from foreign political domination.

In surveying the various techniques used by propagandists in spreading national consciousness and solidarity among the masses, we found that one of these techniques is appeal to common defense against a foreign enemy. Now, defense obviously presupposes aggression; therefore, it is the aggressor, not the defender, who initiates the conflict. Can we explain the origin of any conflict between nationalities by discovering which one acted as aggressor?

Usually this is a controversial issue. While a social conflict is going on, each party generally claims that the other was the aggressor. This is especially true in intergroup conflict, where, as we have noticed, it is easier to gain the cooperation of members for common defense than for common aggression, unless they can be persuaded that aggression is the best means of preventive defense against future aggression. We are familiar with the controversies which arose during and after World War I, as to which sovereign state was the original aggressor, and with the controversy after World War II between those who denounced Russian aggression in Europe and those who claimed that Russia was on the defensive.

However, this problem, though difficult, is not insolvable. It is possible to ascertain objectively whether a particular nationality (or, more exactly, certain organized groups functioning on its behalf) is acting aggressively in relation to some

113

other nationality. This does not necessarily mean that the latter is entirely on the defensive: aggression may be mutual. Nor is a single collective action performed at a particular moment sufficient to decide which group is the aggressor, though when a state declares war or without any declaration starts a military invasion of the territory of another state, political scientists usually judge it to be the aggressor.

Sociologists have to investigate the relationships between the two nationalities during a lengthy period preceding the outbreak of hostilities. And, above all, they should remember that all modern national culture societies (unlike conservative tribal societies and folk communities, exclusive religious sects, and certain stabilized, peaceful states) tend to *expand;* their very formation is a dynamic, expansive process, and their further development depends upon two kinds of expansion.

We may call *creative expansion* that kind which manifests itself in the conscious striving of group members to enrich the national culture by creative activities. As we have seen, it begins with innovations of creative individuals, each of whom gains the support of followers and sponsors, and it gradually leads to the formation of numerous and diverse organized groups which function to promote, multiply, and integrate creative contributions in all realms of culture, ideational and material. The other, universal, type of expansion (connected with the first and discussed in the preceding chapter) may be called *popular expansion.* It consists in purposive efforts to gain new members and thus raise the membership in a national culture society from the relatively small nucleus of intellectuals to the hundreds of thousands or the millions of people who, according to the ethnic standards of historians and ethnologists, should belong to the same cultural society, but as a matter of fact are not yet conscious of belonging. This, as we have seen, is achieved in part by propaganda and in full by organized mass education.

Now, while either creative or popular expansion may encounter the active opposition of religious groups, political groups, and dominant social classes, it does not result in conflicts *between nationalities.* Such conflicts originate only when a particular nationality purposely tends to expand at the cost of another or when two nationalities continue to expand in a way that makes the expansion of one interfere with the expansion of the other. Such expansion may be considered *aggressive.* There are four well-known types of "aggressive" expansion which lead to conflict: *geographic, economic, assimilative,* and *ideological.* If coercion is used in the course of expansion, the conflicts become intensified and frequently result in violent struggles.

Geographic expansion

A social group expands geographically when its members move into areas previously unoccupied or occupied by people who do not belong to it. The migration of group members into new areas is, thus, a necessary condition of geographic expansion, and migration—especially tribal migration into territories already occupied by other tribes—is recognized by historians and archeologists as the oldest source of intergroup struggles.

Not every migration, however, is expansion. If the entire group deserts the area which it previously occupied and moves into another area, this does not mean that its original territory has been enlarged. If only a part of the group membership migrates and the migrants or their descendants cease to maintain social connections with the group of their origin, that group loses members without gaining more land.

Originally, effective geographic expansion was carried on almost exclusively by conquest. A political society expanded geographically when, after it had conquered a new territory, a part of its population moved into this territory and settled there permanently, while remaining members of the conquering state. Geographic expansion without political conquest was first developed by ecclesiastical societies. The Jewish Diaspora is the best known example of this. Migrations of groups of Jews into widely scattered localities within areas inhabited by peoples with diverse cultures and controlled by separate states has been going on for more than twenty centuries, and yet few of these local communities became isolated: some degree of unity was maintained through the advent of travelers and new migrants, later by modern means of communication. The geographic expansion of Christian churches, though often helped by conquest, was mainly achieved by small groups of missionaries who migrated into various territories, sometimes quite distant from their original centers, and organized large groups of converts. Although the territories were controlled by separate states, the social solidarity of all these groups was maintained by a united clergy, not only when the majority of the population of these states became converted, but even when the converts formed only a minority.

Common secular culture as a bond of solidarity between politically separated emigrant groups and the groups from which they came was found in ancient Greece, where colonial city-states preserved some social connections with the city-states of their origin; but, as we know, Greek cultural solidarity was never strong enough to overcome political divisions and conflicts. Only in modern times did migration—sometimes preceded, sometimes followed, by political conquest—become an important force in the expansion of national culture societies and lead sooner or later to conflict between them. The primary source of conflict is, of course, the resistance of the original inhabitants of the land, which they consider their own, against the penetration of "foreigners," especially (as we mentioned before) when the foreigners are conquerors and superimpose their possessive claims to the land upon the claims of "natives." Even when no coercion is used and foreigners are allowed to enter, there is a general tendency to isolate them spatially as

116

well as socially, to treat their settlements as limited "islands," and to prevent them from spreading beyond those limits. These tendencies, as we know, are sometimes reciprocated by the immigrants themselves, who prefer to live together in at least partial territorial isolation.[1] So long as such separatism is accepted by both groups, it does not raise conflicts, but it often facilitates the emergence of conflicts.

Let us survey briefly certain historically significant processes of geographic national expansion in Europe. We omit the many tribal migrations during the first ten centuries of the Christian Era, since these have no direct bearing upon our problem. Later, the expansive trends moved mostly, though not exclusively, in two opposite directions, westward and eastward.

The Tartar invasion of Eastern Europe led to permanent Tartar settlements in the territory along the Volga River and in the Crimea; it was followed by centuries of conflict between the Tartars and the native Russians and Ukrainians. The Turkish conquest of Constantinople and the Balkans resulted in almost continuous conflicts between the Turks and the conquered peoples—Greeks, Serbs, Bulgarians, Rumanians—which did not end until after World War I, when the Turks lost control of all this territory except Istanbul and its neighboring region.[2]

More influential in the long run has been the German expansion eastward from the eleventh century on. It consisted in gradual penetration of migrants from the various regions with traditional German cultures into areas inhabited by Slavs, Prussians, Letts, Estonians. In some cases, it followed military conquests made by emperors, margraves (Austria, Brandenburg), Knights of the Cross, and Knights of the Sword, and eventually met active political and military resistance from Czechs, Poles, Lithuanians. In other cases, the migration was peaceful: German immigrants were welcomed by the rulers and magnates of Bohemia, Poland, and Hungary.[3] For centuries there was no unity and no common nationalistic tendency in

1. Numerous examples of these reciprocal tendencies to isolation may be mentioned: the Jewish ghettos; German settlements in Bohemia, Poland, Transylvania, Russia, especially in rural areas; and foreign immigrant groups in the United States and Brazil.

2. For a short history of Turkish expansion, see George J. Eversley, *The Turkish Empire* (London, 1923).

3. An interesting survey of German expansion in all directions is found in Theodor Arldt, *Germanische Völkerwellen* (Leipzig, 1917). He identifies "Germanic" with "Nordic" and considers the people who call themselves "Deutsche" as a branch of the Germanic race: "Am bekanntesten von den grossen germanischen Völkerwellen ist die deutsche." He devotes one chapter to eastward expansion and another to migration "overseas," especially to the United States. Of course, "die Deutschen" are a great "Volk," with a higher culture, a distinctive way of life, great military and state-building power, superior art and knowledge.

these movements. Toward the second half of the eighteenth century, however, when German nationalism was developing, these movements began to be consistently stimulated, promoted, and organized in the common interest of the German national culture society and eventually conceived as an inherently purposeful, collective *Drang nach Osten*. Consequently, all German expansion became aggressive. This trend culminated in the attempt of the Nazi regime to conquer and occupy permanently Czechoslovakia, Poland, the Ukraine, and the Balkans. No notable westward geographic expansion of non-German nationalities into areas inhabited by Germans occurred until after World War II, when Poles and Czechs expelled Germans and reoccupied some of the territories into which the Germans had migrated during the preceding centuries.

In the middle of the fourteenth century, Polish geographic expansion eastward began. Polish migrants slowly penetrated territories occupied by Western Ukrainians, White Ruthenians, and Lithuanians. Since, during this period, the gentry and some of the urban population in these areas became Polonized, few conflicts resulted from this expansion until the nineteenth century, when Ukrainian and Lithuanian national cultures were revived and national solidarity developed. Here again, after World War II, the trend of expansion was reversed when most of the Poles were compelled to move out of these territories.

Russian geographic expansion has continued throughout many centuries.[4] At first, it was mostly northward into sparsely inhabited areas, with no serious conflicts until the struggle for southern Finland began. In the sixteenth century under Ivan the Great, aggressive colonial expansion eastward started into the Urals and Siberia, and eventually resulted in many minor conflicts as well as in several well-known wars. About two centuries later, southward migrations began toward the Caspian Sea, into Eastern Ukraine, the Caucasus, and the Crimea, also accompanied by conflicts, some of which still persist. Expansion westward was much slower; even after the conquest of eastern

4. Cf. Sir Bernard Pares, A *History of Russia* (New York: Knopf, 1946).

and central Poland, relatively few Russians migrated as permanent settlers into these conquered territories, except nobles to whom the Tsarist government gave confiscated estates of Polish and Lithuanian rebels. However, when Estonia, Latvia, Lithuania, White Ruthenia, and Western Ukraine became finally incorporated into the Soviet Union after World War II, a growing number of Russians began to move into these areas.[5]

We are familiar with the geographic expansion of other European nationalities outside of Europe from the sixteenth century on, usually preceded, accompanied, or followed by conquest. Here, of course, we are not interested in mere political and economic domination of a conquered country by administrative, military, and business groups, such as the British domination of India, with no colonization by permanent settlers. Spanish and Portuguese expansion in South America; English expansion in North America, Australia, New Zealand, South Africa, and certain regions of Central Africa; French expansion in North America and northwestern Africa; and Dutch expansion in South Africa were all definitely geographic in the sense defined above, even though migration of permanent colonists into the conquered territories was sometimes relatively slow.

We need not discuss the numerous, often violent, conflicts between colonists and natives trying to defend their land from foreign invasion. But we must remember that, while this expansion was going on, struggles frequently arose between the expanding nationalities for the occupation and control of the same territories, e.g., between the Spaniards, the English, and the French in North America and, more recently, between the English and the Boers in South Africa. In some areas, after foreign colonization had begun, the revival of old, rather stagnant, national cultures (as in Indonesia and Indo-China) or the emergence of new national cultures (as in Nigeria) resulted in conflicts between these nationalities and the colonial nationalities which had hitherto dominated them.

During the nineteenth century, with the progress of trans-

5. For tentative statistical data on the geographic expansion of the Russian nationality westward since 1939, see Jozef Poniatowski, "Population of the Intermarrium after the Second World War," *The Eastern Quarterly*, Vol. IV, No. 3 (London, July, 1951).

6. The best information is about German immigrants in the United States: Ulrich B. Steuer, "The German National Culture Society in the United States" (manuscript). For an interesting history of the tendency to unification, see Heinz Kloss, *Um die Einigung des Deutschamerikanertums* (Berlin, 1937): Part II, "Kirchliche Einigungsbestrebungen"; Part III, "Geschichte der weltlichen [secular] deutschen Einigungsbestrebungen [from 1819 to 1933]."

7. Cf. *Wir Deutschen in der Welt*, yearly publication of the "Verband der deutschen Vereine im Ausland" (Stuttgart, 1935 ff.). However, the duration of the solidarity among immigrants depends upon their resistance to assimilation. It is significant that the attempt of the Hitler regime to make people of German descent abroad cooperate with the Third Reich was least successful in the United States, judging from the small percentage of such people who joined the German Bund: Emma L. W. Burkhardt, "The Amerika-Deutscher Volksbund" (manuscript).

8. Thus, "The World Union of Poles Abroad" includes Polish associations scattered over all the continents. Since World War II, however, it has no connection with official organizations in Poland, for it is opposed to the present communist government.

portation, communication, writing, and printing, even scattered settlements of emigrants in distant lands who shared the same national culture could remain or become socially united, just like religious settlements. Under such conditions, the potential range of geographic expansion of a numerous, solidary, and well-organized national culture society may extend over every section of the inhabitable surface of the earth where its members can enter as immigrants, and every firmly established local community composed of its members can function on its behalf.

This is well exemplified by the social unification of innumerable German settlements, old and new, scattered all over Europe, the Americas, and the other continents, with the main body of the national society formed by the inhabitants of Germany.[6] This unification was progressively achieved by a great number and variety of local groups, many of which became parts of larger, super-local, associations. These groups had specific primary or secondary functions serving the common interests of the German nationality: transmission of German culture, development in every settlement of conscious solidarity with the national society as a whole, cooperation in German economic expansion, advancement of German prestige, and spread of German influence among other societies.[7] Before World War II, some other nationalities—e.g., the Italians and the Poles—had achieved similar, though not so effective, results.[8]

However, such an integration of foreign immigrant communities of the same nationality is apt to raise conflicts between them and the original inhabitants or earlier settlers of a different nationality, even when the immigrants were at first freely admitted, if not welcomed, as in the United States or Latin America. This is no longer a question of prejudice against foreigners; for if these immigrant groups remain solidary parts of the national culture society from which they come, in any conflict between that society and the one in which they live they may side with the former against the latter. This is the root of

120

the much discussed antagonism of Americans against German immigrants and their descendants during World War I, and the considerable mistrust of Japanese, German, and Italian immigrants during World War II. The anti-Semitism which arose in Poland in the first quarter of this century was mainly due to the assumption (promulgated by nationalistic politicians) that German, Austrian, and Russian Jews were opposed to Polish independence and that the Polish Jews sided with them.

Conflicts become intensified when the society to which the immigrants belong begins to raise territorial claims to the land in which they have settled, and another society whose members also inhabit this land disputes those claims and raises claims of its own. Such was the origin of the struggles for Transylvania—with a mixed German, Magyar, and Rumanian population—after the Ottoman Empire lost control of this territory. First it became a part of Austria, later was ceded by the Hapsburgs to Hungary, to which it had belonged before the Turkish invasions; after World War I, it was incorporated into Rumania. The Rumanians claim that it was inhabited by Rumanians before the Magyars came, and the Magyars claim that Rumanians migrated into it after the Turkish military conquest of central and eastern Hungary.

Another well-known example is the recent struggle for Palestine. For many centuries Palestine was exalted by the Jews in the Diaspora as their own Holy Land, although they had lost it in the first century A.D. and only a small minority of its population remained Jewish. But after the emergence of Zionism, Jewish immigration steadily grew, until Palestine was claimed by Zionists all over the world, not only as the religious center, but as the national land of the Jewish people, descendants of its original inhabitants, with a growing modern national culture rooted in the original culture of Israel. This claim was counteracted by the Arab nationalists of all the states under Arab rule, on the ground that Palestine had been conquered and settled by Arabs long before Jewish immigration started.[9]

9. There is considerable factual evidence that the struggle is nationalistic, not religious: Philip H. Stoddard, "Conflict in Palestine: Judaism vs. Islam? Zionism vs. Arab Nationalism?" (manuscript).

However, the most conspicuous—indeed, historically un-paralleled—example of violent struggles resulting from geographic expansion was the attempt of the Nazi regime to gain control of all the territories where German colonists were settled. The justification of this attempt by Hitler, Goebbels, and other Nazi leaders was the need of liberating Germans outside of Germany from foreign oppression and achieving their complete unification with the Germans in Germany. This implied, first of all, incorporation into the Third Reich of all territories within Europe where Germans lived—Schleswig-Holstein, Transylvania, Czechoslovakia, western Poland, and Alsace-Lorraine—although some compromise was made at first with Russia concerning the Baltic States and with Italy concerning the Tyrol. But plans for the future included control by the Reich of the countries in Latin America with considerable German populations (although here also a compromise was necessary with Mussolini's Italy and Franco's Spain) and of the United States, where according to some Nazi ideologists nearly one-third of the population was of German descent.[10]

10. See, e.g., *Statistischer Handbuch der Volksdeutschen Übersee*, Heinz Kloss, ed. (Stuttgart, 1943). According to what the author considered a moderate calculation, 18,400,000 or 27.5 per cent of the total white population of the United States was "Volksdeutsche." Some earlier calculations were much more optimistic from the German point of view. Thus, according to Emil Mannhart, as early as 1900, 25,477,583 people in the United States were of German descent. The United States should be Germanized, according to Colin Ross, *Unser Amerika* (Leipzig, 1936), because "America has lost faith and ideals" (p. 300). Only if those Americans of German blood become conscious that they ought not give up their *Volkstum* and their mother tongue, will the foundation be laid for a future American *Volk*, or rather a family of *Völker* (p. 301).

Economic expansion

Economic expansion of a social group may be defined as increasing utilization for its own benefit of the material products and the technical actions of members of another group. Such expansion is certainly very old; it has been carried on by both violent and nonviolent methods. Already in some tribal societies warriors periodically entered the territories of neighboring tribes and took some of their economic possessions away. In the early wars between states, invading armies looted the movable property of their enemies, and the more powerful states exacted tribute from the weaker states. These methods continued to be used throughout history and still are being used in aggressive warfare. The primary purpose of the conquistadors was to gain wealth by robbing Amerindians of gold and other valuable possessions. In Europe, looting by invading troops was a long-lasting, widely spread custom, especially in the military expansion of the Turkish Empire; although condemned by international law, it still occurred during World War II. More important, however, in modern times is forcible appropriation by victorious political societies of the valuable possessions of defeated societies. It may appear as outright economic gain, like the appropriation by Nazi Germany of industries in conquered countries, or as compensation for economic losses which the victors incurred during the war, like the compensation imposed upon Germany after World War I or the appropriation by Soviet Russia of industrial machines and products in conquered territories after World War II; but in any case, it is intended to benefit the victors at the cost of the vanquished.

In the utilization of foreign technical actions, or foreign "labor," violent methods have been even more general and more persistent. Coercive importation and enslavement of "foreign" workers began in prehistoric times and has continued up to the present time. During World War II, the Germans and the Russians forced millions of foreigners to work in factories and mines, to cultivate land, or to build roads. Serfdom, in the sense of gaining by force mastery of productive land and compelling its inhabitants to give some products and services to masters and their descendants, lasted until the middle of the nineteenth century and, as peonage, survived until recently in some Latin American countries.

However, nonviolent methods of acquiring foreign products in exchange for the products of one's own society and of inducing foreigners to work by economic rewards, much more effective in the long run than violent methods, developed rapidly in the course of history and predominate in modern times.[11] Modern economic expansion was one result of the growth of

11. This type of expansion is well known, and so many works have been published about it that no references are needed here. We might mention, however, by way of example, Frank Herbert Simons, *The Great Powers in World Politics; International Relations and Economic Nationalism*, 3d ed. (New York: American Book, 1939).

organized capitalism and the technical progress of industry, especially since the beginning of the eighteenth century. But this was also the period when national solidarity based on common culture grew. National societies with well-organized capitalistic systems and advanced industries began to expand by gaining economic control over the products, labor, and natural resources of technologically and economically backward societies, so as to increase their own wealth. In the course of this expansion, conflicts naturally arose between the expanding society and the society over which it was trying to gain economic control, as well as between societies which were expanding within the same area.

When economic expansion of European nationalities outside of Europe began, some competition between them arose; but so long as there were many opportunities for expansion in new territories, conflicts could be avoided. Thus, in the sixteenth century, the areas of potential Spanish and Portuguese expansion were separated by common agreement; and in the nineteenth century, when China became accessible to the economic expansion of Western nationalities, a compromise was reached between them. But with the tremendous development of industrial production, especially in countries where it had been lagging, the growing need of new markets for exports and of raw materials for imports brought increasing conflicts. Thus, the growth of German industry and organized foreign trade led to an economic expansion of the German national society which was particularly rapid in eastern Europe and Latin America, slower but still effective in some areas of Asia and Africa, and which resulted in growing conflicts with the British, the French, and more recently the American society.

Economic expansion was usually initiated by private associations, but sooner or later state governments gave it political support, usually under the pressure of industrialists, merchants, and bankers. This is, for instance, what the British government did in India, in China, and in South Africa; and the German

124

imperial government, in southeastern Europe and western Asia. Such support has often been an important factor of the political conflicts between expanding nationalities which culminated in wars; but seldom, if ever, the only factor. We should not exaggerate its importance, as economic determinists of various schools are doing. For instance, although the Japanese struggle for the domination of eastern Asia was strongly influenced by the tendency to economic expansion, the influence of political imperialism and of aggressive cultural nationalism was indubitable.

Conflict between an economically expanding nationality and a nationality subjected to this expansion not only implies that participants in the latter are aware of the foreign domination, but requires some degree of social solidarity in counteracting this domination. The consciousness of being dominated develops whenever foreigners have penetrated into an area occupied by another nationality and assumed control of certain activities of the natives. Thus, when foreign merchants and associations of merchants settle in commercial centers, import foreign products, and export native products, both consumers and producers come to depend upon them. The domination is even more obvious when foreign capitalists acquire and exploit natural resources—arable land, forests, mines, oil wells—and when industrialists organize factories, employ native labor under foreign management. The opposition usually turns first against those dominating foreign individuals and groups and tends to control their functions for the benefit of the native population, if not to expropriate them. Such was originally the opposition against "North American capitalists" in Latin American countries. And Sun Yat-sen's appeal to Chinese solidarity against foreign—especially British—economic domination was primarily based on this kind of opposition.

Eventually, however, nationalistic leaders and groups try to develop the industrial production of their own nationality and to counteract the importation and use of foreign products. This

125

is an impersonal, strictly economic competition, though social methods may be used to achieve its purposes. If the nationality controls an independent state, groups of producers exert pressure upon the government to prohibit or limit foreign imports by tariffs. In recent times, as economic, political, and military struggles between nationally dominated states increased, this tendency culminated in the ideal of "autarchy," complete technical and economic self-sufficiency of an organized and politically independent national culture society. If the political power of a state which promotes the export of products of its own nationality prevents the use of this defensive method— e.g., in India during British rule or in China when powerful Western states made prohibitive or even high taxation of their products impossible—other methods have been used, such as boycott of foreign products by potential consumers. The efficiency of this method requires, of course, a high degree of spontaneous national solidarity and strong opposition to foreign control. The boycott of British products by Hindus on the initiative of Gandhi is a well-known example.

Assimilative expansion

The third type of aggressive expansion of nationalities is a continuation of what we called "popular expansion," that is, the spreading of national culture and solidarity among the masses. It consists in the cultural assimilation and incorporation into a nationality of people who by ethnic standards are not supposed to belong to it. We may, therefore, call it "assimilative expansion." It is intended, first of all, to increase the size of the nationality, but also to overcome whatever separatism may have existed between it and the ethnically different group by absorbing the latter. When the people who are being assimilated already belong to another nationality, their assimilation means that the latter is in danger of losing a part of its present and future members. Consequently, such attempts at assimilative expansion provoke active resistance and result in social conflicts.

Conflicts may also arise when two nationalities compete in trying to assimilate the same people, who do not belong to either. Analogous conflicts have existed for many centuries between ecclesiastic societies whose membership is not limited in advance by alleged common descent, but can indefinitely increase by gaining new converts. We may mention, for instance, conflicts between expanding Christian groups and the older religious groups during the second, third, and fourth centuries of the Christian Era, later between Christians and Moslems, between Protestants and Catholics in Europe, and between Christians of various denominations trying to convert "pagans" outside of Europe.

However, there is a difference between religious conversion and national assimilation. An individual cannot participate at the same time in two different religions; whereas an individual who participates in the culture of one nationality can also participate in the culture of another, while being loyal to only one of them or partly loyal to both. What we call national "assimilation" means, therefore, not only transmitting to ethnic foreigners a national culture, but imparting to them exclusive national loyalty to it, preventing them from remaining loyal to the nationality whose culture they originally shared or from developing a divided loyalty—especially when there is a conflict between the two nationalities.

Several methods may be used in the course of assimilative expansion to achieve its purpose. The separate organizations of "foreigners" are often dissolved; further participation in their original culture is apt to be impeded and the prestige of this culture lowered by invidious propaganda; sometimes even the culture is purposely destroyed.

Since assimilation requires some education, formal or informal, both in acquiring a new culture and in learning a new loyalty, education has always been used as the main method of assimilative expansion, especially by the dominant nationality within a large state which includes other nationalities. Such a dominant nationality obviously has a considerable advantage. It can organize schools on all levels, transmitting its culture to subordinate nationalities, appropriate or abolish whatever schools the latter may have, and prevent them from organizing other schools to transmit their cultures.

This is how Austria carried on assimilation of the Czechs, and later of the Poles, until cultural autonomy was granted to them in 1866, and how in Hungary the Slovaks were being assimilated by the Magyars. In Prussia during the second half of the nineteenth century, school education was conducted in German and thus served to assimilate all non-German subjects. In Tsarist Russia attempts to absorb peoples of other nationalities into the dominant "Great Russian" nationality by education in universities, gymnasiums (secondary schools), and primary schools, began under Nicholas I and by the end of the nineteenth century were consistently carried on throughout the empire.

Such assimilative expansion with the aid of political power always meets opposition. We have already mentioned by way of example the resistance of Poles to coercive Russification and Germanization. Even when Russian or German culture was thoroughly imparted to them, this did not make the Poles loyal Russians or Germans. Far from it. The same can be said of other nationalities in Tsarist Russia, of Czechs in Austria, and of Slovaks in Hungary. Indeed, such coercive assimilation of subordinate nationalities has been one of the main factors in their striving for political independence.

Other conflicts due to assimilative expansion emerged during the nineteenth century in so-called "border areas," whose mixed populations shared different national cultures with peoples outside of their borders: Alsace (French and German), the Southern Tyrol (Austrian-German and Italian), the northern

128

shore of the Adriatic (South Slavic and Italian), Macedonia (Greek, Serb, and Bulgarian). Any tendency of one of these nationalities to assimilate and absorb all the inhabitants of such an area provoked active opposition of the other nationality; and eventually each of them attempted to get control of the whole area so as to carry on its own assimilative expansion.

Thus, in Alsace-Lorraine French national culture slowly expanded from the time of the French Revolution until 1870 without the use of coercive methods. After 1871, the systematic compulsory Germanization of this area by education was carried on. Following the Versailles Treaty, the French began to educate or re-educate the Alsatians in French culture and loyalty. This trend was reversed in 1940 and has been reversed again since 1945. Italianization of the Slavs in the province of Venetia Giulia was thoroughly carried on under the Fascist regime,[12] but after the Italian defeat in World War II, the opposite tendency appeared. We mentioned above the struggles between Magyars and Rumanians for control of Transylvania, where both nationalities lived. These struggles were closely connected with the growing tendencies of both to assimilative expansion.[13]

Somewhat different are the conflicts which result when two nationalities tend to assimilate people who ethnically do not belong to either. The century-old conflict between Great Russians and Poles, who were separated by vast regions inhabited by Lithuanians, White Ruthenians, and Ukrainians, was partly due to attempts of Poles to Polonize and of Russians to Russify these peoples. The peaceful Polonization of the gentry and the higher urban classes in these areas proceeded gradually from the middle of the sixteenth to the latter part of the eighteenth century. Russification began soon after the partition of Poland, but because of the use of coercive methods was not very successful, except on the eastern border.[14] After the western section of this territory became again a part of Poland (in 1920), the census showed that less than one per cent of the population

12. Cf. Lavo Cermelj, *Life-and-Death Struggle of a National Minority* (Ljubljana, 1930).

13. The Flemish movement within Belgium in opposition to the culturally, though not economically, dominant Walloons had a somewhat similar origin. Cf. Clough Sheppard, *A History of the Flemish Movement in Belgium* (London, 1916); Jules Destrée, *Wallons et Flamands* (Paris, 1923). The opposition of French Canadians to British Canadians also arose, at least in part, in consequence of the tendency of the British to cultural, as well as economic, domination. Cf. William Henry Moore, *The Clash. A Study in Nationalities* (New York: Dutton, 1919).

14. Cf. Adam Zoltowski, *Border of Europe, A Study of the Polish Eastern Provinces* (London, 1950).

considered themselves Russians. The Poles soon tried to Polonize the lower classes in these areas by education. But by then Ukrainian, Lithuanian, and partly White Ruthenian national cultures had already developed. Consequently, conflicts emerged between those nationalities and the Poles. After Russia reconquered these territories in 1939, the same nationalities again began to struggle against the Russians.

We are familiar with the cultural assimilation of foreign immigrants which has been going on for thousands of years. This was originally a gradual, unplanned, rather spontaneous process, especially if no religious differences were involved. It depended, and still depends, on social contacts between immigrants and "natives." Where immigrants formed isolated groups, assimilation might be very slow: for instance, in Transylvania German settlers preserved their culture for six hundred years. Even now immigrant settlers in rural areas maintain their culture longer than those who settle in cities. A second important factor is the cultural level of the people among whom the immigrants settle. The more developed the aboriginal culture, the more influential it is. Even foreign conquerors are often assimilated, as shown by the gradual Latinization of the Franks, Lombards, Visigoths, and Normans.

The growth of modern national cultures made the spontaneous assimilation of foreign immigrants faster and more effective. Thus, as Polish national culture grew from the sixteenth century on, the descendants of German settlers in urban areas became assimilated at an increasingly rapid rate, contributing more and more to its further growth. The dynamic development of American culture also resulted in speeding up the process of spontaneous assimilation of immigrants and their participation in this development; [15] whereas in Latin American countries, so long as their cultures remained relatively stagnant, the assimilation of immigrants was much slower.

However, such spontaneous assimilation has sometimes

15. Considerable information about the assimilation of immigrants is contained in such works as Francis J. Brown and Joseph S. Roucek, eds., One America (New York: Prentice-Hall, Inc., 1945); Louis Adamic, A Nation of Nations (New York: Harper, 1944); R. A. Schermerhorn, These Our People (Boston: Heath, 1949). An excellent selected bibliography has been published by the U. S. Dept. of Justice (Washington, D. C.: Immigration and Naturalization Service, 1948). Significant data about assimilation are contained in life histories of immigrants: Helen L. Norris, "Voluntary Americanization of Immigrants as Shown through Autobiographies" (manuscript).

been impeded by opposing nationalistic trends which produced social conflicts. Immigrant groups actively resist assimilation whenever they wish to remain socially united with the
nationality of their origin and purposely try to maintain their
own distinct national culture and solidarity. We mentioned before how such groups can be and have been used by the society
from which they came, when the latter is involved in a struggle
with the nationality in whose territory the immigrants have
settled. But even when there is no such struggle, the nationality
which dominates the immigrants politically tends to overcome
their resistance by imposing its own culture and loyalty upon
them. This is best done by public education, which does not
necessarily provoke conflicts, so long as immigrant groups are
left free to organize schools for the transmission of their own
culture to the young generation. But if such schools are prohibited, conflicts arise.

A very different and more serious kind of conflict emerges
when a dominant nationality, though imparting its own culture
to ethnic "foreigners," does not admit them to participation as
full members, because it considers them racially inferior. While
European rulers in colonial territories transmitted some of their
culture to a minority of natives, the purpose was to facilitate
their rule, not to increase the size of their own nationality by
incorporating those foreigners, since the latter were usually
considered hereditarily unfit to become full members of the
dominant society.

Such interference of racial prejudice with the tendency to assimilative expansion was most clearly manifested under the
Nazi regime. Instead of trying to make Germans out of conquered Poles, Czechs, Yugoslavs, as the Austrians and Prussians
had done under the imperial regimes, the Nazis wanted to
incorporate only "Volksdeutsche," descendants of Germans, and
treated those who were not of German origin as racially unfit
to participate fully in German culture and be admitted into
the German society. On the other hand, the Nazi regime did

not want these foreigners to preserve their own cultures, since they were destined to become servants of the Herrenvolk, helping to develop German culture. Consequently, the systematic destruction of these foreign cultures began, while only enough German culture was imparted to them to make them serve efficiently.

In other cases, a compromise was sought between the tendency to assimilative expansion and the unwillingness to admit inferior people to full membership. The inferiors became incorporated into the national society, but separatism was preserved by treating them as a lower hereditary class or caste. Such was, for instance, the original attitude of "100% Americans" toward immigrants from Eastern and Southern Europe and their descendants. It was somewhat analogous to the prevalent attitude of Southerners toward culturally Americanized Negroes. Such treatment inevitably results in conflicts which interfere with national solidarity.

Ideological expansion

When nationalistic leaders develop certain ideals of social order and cultural progress and assume that it is their task or "mission" to have these ideals accepted and applied by leaders of other nationalities, this is the beginning of another kind of expansion which eventually results in conflict.

For instance, French ideologists of the eighteenth century tried with some success to have their ideals accepted by social thinkers and even rulers of other nationalities; but, after the Revolution, when French leaders with the support of French armies attempted to introduce these ideals into foreign countries, their attempts intensified the violent struggles between the French Republic and the societies with dominant monarchical ideologies. The much discussed conflicts between "the West" and "the East" were due not only to the aggressive economic expansion of Western nationalities, but also to their attempts to introduce into the countries which they dominated their own conceptions of social order and their own ideals of cultural progress, although they disagreed in many respects with the cultural standards and norms which the people in those countries considered valid.

The general principle underlying the ideological expansion of a national culture society (just like the missionary efforts of a religious society) is the belief that this society is culturally superior to others and that consequently its intellectual leaders are supreme authoritative judges in cultural matters: they know better than anybody else what is right and what is wrong, what ought to be done to maintain and improve social order and to promote progress in such realms of culture as technology, economic organization, science, even art and literature. Their authority ought to be recognized and their guidance followed by leaders of other nationalities. If it is not recognized or if the subordinate leaders have no ability or power to realize the ideals as conceived by their authoritative superiors, coercion must be employed. This presupposes, of course, that the supreme authorities have sufficient power at their disposal.

In the modern world, however, most national societies with distinctive cultures are considered by their leaders as capable of progress without foreign authoritative guidance. But, on the other hand, several nationalities are judged by their own intellectual elite to be superior to others, and each of them assumes the task of guiding others toward progress. Moreover, the ideologies of progress of the authoritative elite differ considerably, as do their standards of right and wrong. Consequently, we find on the one hand conflicts between nationalities which attempt to impose their authoritative leadership upon others and those nationalities which resist such attempts and, on the other hand, wider conflicts between nationalities with divergent ideologies, each of which has assumed the mission of spreading its ideology.

We might discuss here several recent attempts at ideological expansion, e.g., the German attempt, which failed for the obvious reason that the German authoritative thinkers supporting the Nazi regime recognized only the German "race" as capable of realizing the ideal of cultural progress, or the ideal of "Asiatic unity" which the Japanese attempted to realize and which failed because its realization conflicted not only with Western expansion, but with the national ideals of other cultural societies in Eastern Asia. We might also survey the present American effort to spread the ideal of democratic freedom as the only way to universal progress.

But nothing in history equals the ideological expansion of Soviet Russia, and its steady growth is most instructive. It began, of course, as an expansion of communism within the realm of Tsarist Russia under the guidance of the Bolshevik Party. According to the basic principles of the Marxian ideology as interpreted by his dogmatic followers, material culture forms the foundation of all culture; social solidarity is ultimately based on common economic interests, and economic conflicts are the main source of all social conflicts; conflicts in the modern world are essentially due to the development of capitalism; within every capitalistic society, the basic struggle is that between the capitalist class and the proletariat class; political and military struggles between states are rooted in struggles between the capitalists who control their governments; and the elimination of the capitalist class would stop both the conflicts within each society and the conflicts between societies. This doctrine either ignores the existence of social solidarity based on common ideational culture or explains it as a by-product of economic forces. In any case, to counteract national conflicts, the best method, as formulated in the Communist Manifesto, is to appeal to the common interest of the "proletarians of all countries" against the capitalists of all countries.

Now, Bolshevik leaders were well aware of the failure of the Tsarist regime to Russify other nationalities and of the striving of those nationalities for independence from Russian domination. They therefore proclaimed the principle of self-determination; every nationality would be granted complete autonomy.[16] But the main goal of the Bolshevik regime was to integrate all the nationalities within the empire into one communist society. To achieve this integration as rapidly as possible, political and military power had to be used, and this power was vested in the Russian nationality. Though the Communist Party included individual members of various nationalities, the majority of them were Russians; and the territory from which the party originally recruited most of its followers was inhabited by Russians.

When the Bolsheviks attempted to gain political and economic control over countries inhabited by other nationalities, their attempts appeared to the latter as a revival of the old nationalistic Russian domination and provoked active resistance, notwithstanding appeals to class solidarity. The resistance of Ukrainians (including peasants) in 1919 led to violent struggles. The Polish insurrection against Tsarist Russia, started in 1914, continued after the Bolshevik Revolution and remained a purely nationalistic war. The Bolshevik invasion of Poland in 1920 met the active resistance of Poles of all classes, as another "Russian" invasion. With the Russian defeat, Poland gained complete separation from Russia. Lithuanians, Letts, and Estonians, mostly peasants and workers, who had struggled for a long time against the upper classes (mostly Poles and Germans, with relatively few Russians) broke away from Russia and with the support of the Western powers formed independent democratic republics. The Bolshevik government opposed this separatism, but was still too weak to prevent it, though not too weak to bring Georgia back into the fold when it tried to form a separate national state.

During the last twenty years, the expansion of communism and that of the Russian national society have been so closely connected that it is difficult to decide which is now the main

16. Joseph Stalin, *Marxism and the National and Colonial Question. Selected Writings and Speeches* (London, 1942). For the actual application of this doctrine, see, e.g., Hans Kohn, *Nationalism and the Soviet Union* (London, 1933); David J. Dallin, *The Rise of Russia in Asia* (New Haven: Yale University Press, 1949).

goal of the Russian communists. Of course, to those who consider that it is the "mission" of the Russian people to spread communism over the world, the two are inseparable. Otherwise why should Russians continue to dominate nationalities whose leaders have already been converted to communism?

One thing is certain: Russian communists are well aware that they must rely on the national loyalty, not merely on the class solidarity, of the 110 million Russian people, both in defense against foreign aggression (as during the German invasion) and in aggressive expansion. This is why the same methods are being used in developing and maintaining the national solidarity of Russians as have been used in other national culture societies, much more effectively than in Tsarist Russia and almost as effectively as in Nazi Germany.

The present Russian method of dealing with subordinate nationalities, not only those already incorporated in the Soviet Union but also those in satellite countries, is a combination of positive encouragement of their own national solidarity, as long as they are willing to cooperate fully with the Russians and follow the guidance of Russian leaders, and of ruthless repression of any nationalistic tendencies which lead to resistance or rebellion against Russian domination.

Thus, after the Russian invasion of Eastern Poland in 1939, Ukrainians, White Ruthenians, and Lithuanians were supported against the Poles, who were expected to oppose the Russian conquest; more than a million Polish inhabitants of all classes were sent to northern Russia and Siberia, thousands of Polish war prisoners were killed. After the war, large areas of eastern Poland became integral parts of the Ukraine, White Ruthenia, and Lithuania. To compensate the Poles for these losses the Russians supported their claims to the whole territory east of the Oder and the Neisse rivers, on the ground that this territory was originally Polish; the German inhabitants were compelled to leave, and it was promptly occupied by Polish

136

settlers. Russians also gave support to the Czechs who expelled Germans from the Sudeten area. Consequently the Poles and the Czechs are expected to cooperate with the Russians in any struggle against the Western powers, especially if the latter should insist on returning those territories to the Germans.

This support of Lithuanian, White Ruthenian, Ukrainian, Polish, and Czech nationality interests was seemingly based on the principle of national self-determination—the same principle which guided the allied powers after World War I. Each nationality was granted political independence.

In order to prevent struggles between nationalities over areas with mixed population (which the League of Nations failed to prevent), the Russians used an apparently easy and definite solution: national boundaries were made coextensive with state boundaries by compulsory mass migrations, so that the total population of every state became homogeneous in culture.

However, national self-determination under Russian guidance does not last long. Not only nationalities already incorporated into the Soviet Union, but all those within the range of Russian military power, have been subjected to increasing Russian domination. Millions of Ukrainian rebels, suspected rebels, and potential rebels against Russian rule were liquidated or transferred to Siberia before World War II, and violent repression of nonconformity was resumed after the war. Since Lithuania, Latvia, and Estonia were reconquered, their control by Russia has been much more strict than it was under the Tsarist regime.

The introduction of communist governments into Poland, Rumania, Bulgaria, Hungary, Czechoslovakia, and eastern Germany followed the penetration of Russian armies into these countries and was carried on under political control directly or indirectly enforced by military power. Many of the communists who govern these countries were trained in Moscow, and all of them were expected to accept unconditionally the supreme authority of Russian communist rulers and to follow their guidance obediently.

First of all, they have to reorganize their societies politically and economically according to communist principles, as interpreted and applied by Stalin and his Russian collaborators; they must also carry on mass propaganda and assume complete control of education. Not only is Russia supposed to be far in advance of other countries in the realization of the communist ideal, but Russian intellectual achievements in every realm of culture—theoretic and applied sciences, literature, art, music—if approved by the Russian government, are exalted as models for other nationalities to imitate.

If the subordinate rulers and leaders in satellite countries meet active resistance, Russian forces help them repress it; but if they deviate from the principles imposed by the supreme Russian authorities, they lose their leadership or are eliminated. And any attempt to make a nationality independent of Russian domination is counteracted by force or threat of force, even if this nationality has already accepted the communist ideal and is trying to realize it. When the German autonomous republic on the Volga was eliminated in 1941 and the Tartar republic of the Crimea in 1945, it was certainly not for economic reasons; nor is the present conflict between Russia and Yugoslavia a struggle between communism and capitalism.

Russian ideological expansion beyond the area actually subjected to Russian political and military domination cannot employ violent methods; nevertheless, it is extremely effective. Every Communist Party throughout the world, no matter to what nationality its members belong, is expected by the ruling Russian communist group to accept its supreme authority and to follow loyally its guidance; and most of them do. Any individual deviation from the narrow, though not always straight, path to the righteousness periodically blueprinted by Stalin's group is a mortal sin; the deviant is branded as a heretic and excommunicated from the fold of the faithful, unless he confesses his error and submits to corrective re-education.

How can violent conflicts between nationalities be prevented?

Since the beginning of this century, when social thinkers became aware of the power of cultural nationalism as a source of conflict, plans have been made to prevent such conflicts from culminating in war. The League of Nations and later the United Nations were instituted to realize these plans. Inasmuch as the modern state has practically a monopoly of the effective use of physical force, such plans are primarily concerned with preventing states from starting war or with stopping it when started. They are drawn up by political scientists and put into action by statesmen. They are generally based on comparative studies of wars and their presumed causes: first, the direct causes immediately preceding the outbreak of war; next, the processes which began in a more distant past and finally culminated in war. This approach, however, leads to a vast multiplicity and diversity of causal factors—ideological, ethnological, political, economic (usually overemphasized), demographic, anthropogeographic—and considerable disagreement as to their relative importance. As a matter of fact, because of the inadequate sociological study of national culture societies and the old tendency to identify them with political societies, political scientists and economists still underestimate the influence of nationalities as such. We have tried to show that in the long run their influence upon state governments is nowadays greater than that of all other groups. Insofar as in their struggles against other nationalities they exert their influence in order to gain control of the coercive methods monopolized by the state, this influence is the main factor in interstate and civil wars.

On the other hand, however, many conflicts between national culture societies have gone on for lengthy periods without recourse to violence and eventually subsided altogether. Why? What are the factors which eliminated those conflicts or at least prevented them from growing worse? This problem has been neglected, and yet it is of primary importance for the effective realization of any attempt to prevent violent struggles.

The failure of the League of Nations to maintain peace was in a considerable measure due to the fact that its leaders knew little about national culture societies and their relationships; consequently, only ineffective attempts were made to counteract the growing conflicts between these societies. Whatever plans for world peace the organizers and leaders of the United Nations have drawn up imply the assumption that they can foresee the future and predict how their plans will be realized. But prediction of the future must be based on adequate knowledge of the present and the past; and however adequate may be our knowledge of political societies, our knowledge of national culture societies, though more advanced than it was thirty years ago, is still far from sufficient.

We see no reason whatever to anticipate that the inner solidarity and expansive tendencies of national culture societies will decrease in the near future. Nor can we expect that conflicts between them will cease to affect the political relations between states, so long as governments are composed of and supported by people who have been indoctrinated and educated for loyal membership in their respective nationalities. The only way of preventing such conflicts from interfering with the formation of any peaceful political world organization or disrupting it after it has been formed is to counteract directly or indirectly those national tendencies which are apt to culminate eventually in violent struggle.

How can this be done in the future? To answer this question we have to search for factual evidence showing how it was actually done in the past and is being done right now. To guide

140

us in this search, we shall use the following hypothesis, which is based on the results reached by those sociologists who have been investigating active relationships between various kinds of social groups: *active intergroup conflicts are effectively inhibited only by active intergroup cooperation.* Mutual isolation has no lasting effect and is impossible in the modern world. Nor does repression of antagonistic conduct by external powers eliminate antagonistic tendencies. We must, therefore, survey comparatively all kinds of active cooperation, not only between national culture societies as wholes, but also between the many specific groups functioning on their behalf.

six

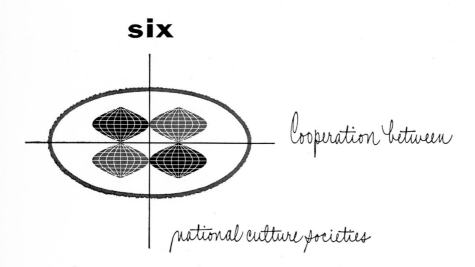

Cooperation between

national culture societies

Defensive cooperation

Of all types of cooperation between societies the most obvious, and the most frequently studied by historians and statesmen, is cooperation for defense against a common enemy.

As we have seen, the inner solidarity of a group is indubitably strengthened by presumed need of defense against a presumably dangerous enemy. In those instances which we discussed, each group or at least its intellectual nucleus was already united by a common bond, religious or national; the enemy was an infidel or a foreigner who endangered important values of the group. It is difficult to unite for common defense two or more societies, religious or national, which have no such bond, but on the contrary may be already activated by mutual antagonism. In such cases there must be indeed a powerful common enemy, against whom neither of these societies alone can defend itself, and an imminent danger of violent aggression threatening both (or all) of them, which can be overcome only by some kind of political and, eventually, military cooperation. Even after cooperation has been initiated, it lasts only as long as the danger lasts.

For instance, common defensive opposition against the Ottoman Empire did occasionally produce a certain amount of cooperation between the diverse ethnic groups within Central–East Europe, which were either subjected to Turkish domination or threatened by Turkish invasion. But no common defensive aim could counteract for long the struggles between the various nationalities inhabiting the Balkan area. Although in recent times some ideologists promulgated the ideal of political unification of these nationalities as the only effective defense of their independence against German imperialistic aggression, on the one hand, and Russian imperialistic aggression, on the other hand, such unification proved impossible in the face of the strong conflicts between them.

The present political cooperation of communist-dominated

nationalities is obviously not based on any necessity for common defense against capitalistic warmongers, since all active aggression has been initiated by the communists. Insofar as cooperation between their ruling groups is voluntary, it is rooted in the common goal of developing and maintaining communism and in more or less effective attempts to improve the relations, especially economic, between nationalities already organized in conformity with the communist pattern. Whether this solidarity will be strong enough to counteract conflicts within each nationality due to the use of violent coercion by communist rulers in controlling their subjects, as well as conflicts between the Russian communist rulers and their puppet rulers in the subordinate nationalities, only the future will show.

The cooperation of nationalities opposed to communism in defense against communist aggression has only begun to develop and, as we know, is still greatly impeded by national separatism and mutual mistrust. It may become strong enough to postpone for awhile another world war; but it can obviously contribute little, if anything, to permanent world unity unless guided by a common positive ideal.

Cultural cooperation

Entirely different, less conspicuous, but in the long run much more influential, is positive cooperation between nationalities in specific realms of culture. This has been slowly, but steadily, increasing during the last century and a half. Although recently cooperation of nationalities inside the communist block with nationalities outside it has decreased, it has not quite stopped yet. Nor is its future increase excluded, for it does not necessarily conflict with the positive ideological principles of communism. If communist rulers are now obstructing it, this is not for ideological reasons, only because

144

they consider cultural isolation of their subjects essential for the preservation of their authority and power.

We shall try to show that the primary source of the social forces which lead to cooperation between national culture societies and which counteract conflicts is their *general tendency toward creative cultural expansion.*

To begin with, historical evidence indicates that, insofar as the activities of a national culture society are directed toward the creative development of its own culture, its aggressive tendencies against other societies seem to become less active: Sweden during the last hundred years (compared with the seventeenth century) and Turkey during the last thirty years are significant examples. On the other hand, when aggressive expansion increases, creative expansion decreases: e.g., German literature, art, music, philosophy, sociology, jurisprudence ceased to develop during the Nazi regime.

Furthermore, we observe that the creative growth of a national culture does not normally provoke other societies to antagonistic activities, though it may stir up rivalry in striving for prestige. It has been and is, increasingly, becoming a factor of positive rather than of negative mutual interest between nationalities. This interest increases in the measure in which national societies utilize results of the creative work done by other societies for their own further development.

Of course, the enrichment of a particular culture by the importation of values and patterns from other cultures is a very old and familiar phenomenon. What is relatively new is the use made of these values and patterns. Instead of being merely incorporated with adaptations into the culture of the society which imports them, they are converted into materials and instruments for the dynamic growth of its culture.

This is a type of creative *cultural fertilization* characteristic of national cultures. It becomes cultural *cross-fertilization* when each of two (or more) societies uses some creative products of the other to promote the growth of its culture. Finally, it leads to

145

cooperative creativeness when leaders of several societies accept some common goal or ideal and act together for its realization. Usually, it began between two nationalities and gradually extended to others. It has also expanded spatially: while at first long distances impeded it, the tremendous advance in means of transportation and communication has made possible cooperation of nationalities inhabiting widely different areas. What is most important, although originally carried on by individual leaders, in the course of time creative cultural fertilization has been taken over by numerous and diverse organized social groups and consequently is becoming increasingly influential.

Interindividual cooperation

Creative fertilization of modern national cultures involved at first only unorganized social cooperation between individual intellectuals of various national societies. Such cooperation was simply a continuation of the intercourse which already existed between medieval cultural leaders in Western and Central Europe who lived and worked in various cultural centers and communicated with each other through travel and correspondence. Since these medieval leaders shared the same religious culture and all used the Latin language, cooperation between them was relatively easy. Though it became more difficult when different national cultures developed, with separate languages, yet it did not stop.

Thus, when influential secular patrons invited prominent foreign architects, sculptors, and painters to work for them, "native" artists sometimes opposed such competition; and yet the personal example of those gifted foreigners usually promoted the growth of national art. For instance, the Italian and, later, the French artists imported by the kings of Poland stimulated the development of Polish art; and Russian secular art

146

grew under the influence of foreign artists imported by the tsars. But considerable cooperation between artists of different nationalities developed independently of their patrons. Young artists went abroad—and still do—to study under famous masters. Some Italian, German, Dutch, French, and Spanish artists in the sixteenth and seventeenth centuries became acquainted with each other's products and often established personal contacts. When musicians began to play the works of foreign composers, this was frequently a result of personal intercourse between them.

Translation of foreign literary works—very important for cultural fertilization—was also initiated by individual men of letters who wanted to make these works available to the reading public of their own society. Often, though not always, it was accompanied by some personal contact between the author, if still alive, and the translator.

Best known is interindividual cooperation in the domain of knowledge. Scientists, scholars, and philosophers of various nationalities met during their travels, exchanged information and criticism concerning their works, and corresponded with each other sometimes throughout years; a vast amount of such correspondence has been published by biographers and historians. There were, of course, linguistic difficulties, unless Latin was still used, but eventually most scientists and scholars learned one or more foreign languages, at least enough to understand works in their own fields. Young scholars and scientists have for centuries gone abroad in order to work under the guidance of the most famous foreign leaders and to learn their methods.

Most of these intellectuals acted as individuals, not as representatives of their nationalities. Nonetheless, their contacts were, and still are, frequently the beginnings of organized international cooperation.

Social groups using foreign creative activities to fertilize their own national cultures

1. Importation of foreign products. This is an old and well-known method in the realm of material culture. Instruments and machines invented by foreign technologists are imported by economic associations or governmental groups to be used for the development of industry or agriculture. However, the *export* of such instruments and machines is apt to meet opposition on the part of economic groups of the nationality which produces them, if these groups fear that the technological progress of the importing nationality will result in competition detrimental to their own interests. This opposition can be overcome only by some kind of economic cooperation between the two nationalities.

But when a national group imports foreign cultural products to promote the creative growth of its own *ideational* culture, it does not meet such opposition on the part of the other nationality. What opposition there is usually comes from some members of its own nationality.

Take the functions of a modern library. Though still primarily devoted to the preservation of domestic literary products and their use for the education and self-education of the native population, the groups which maintain and run libraries have been increasing the importation of foreign publications which are presumably valuable enough to be used for the creative growth of their national culture.[1] This has been done chiefly on the initiative of specialists in various realms who need continuous acquaintance with the results of foreign intellectual activity. It is sometimes impeded by ideologists who do not want the literary works of foreigners whose ideologies disagree with their own to be made accessible to readers of their nationality.[2]

In the realm of plastic arts, national artistic associations were at first reluctant to admit the works of foreign artists to the exhibitions of art which they periodically arranged. Such

1. Take, for instance, the Bibliothèque Nationale (originally Bibliothèque Royale) in Paris, the Library of the British Museum in London, the Berlin State Library, the Library of the Vatican, the United States Library of Congress, the New York Public Library. Most of the libraries of scientific associations, as well as university libraries, throughout the world import or exchange foreign books.

2. Thus, the importation of foreign books by libraries was censored in Russia during some periods of the Tsarist regime, in Germany during the Nazi regime, and is being censored now in the Soviet Union and satellite countries.

exclusiveness lasted in Paris and London almost to the end of the nineteenth century. But in modern times, the expanding function of museums is to contribute to the creative fertilization of national art. Museums quite early included the products of artists of several nationalities, though at first only works of artists long dead. Gradually, however, relatively recent works and finally even the products of living foreign artists were admitted to certain museums, mostly on the initiative of groups of patrons and connoisseurs, with the result that artists, prospective artists, and amateurs became positively interested in the contemporary creative development of art in other cultural societies.

2. Invitations extended to foreign cultural leaders. The earliest type of organized cultural cooperation which was initiated by social groups in order to promote the development of their national culture was the invitation of intellectually prominent foreigners to participate in their activities and to communicate to their members new cultural products and patterns.

National universities and other centers of higher education have long been accustomed to import permanently or for a limited time foreign scholars and scientists whose functions as teachers and creative leaders were expected to contribute to the creative growth of the cultures which the universities maintained and developed. This was merely a continuation, or rather a revival, of the custom of medieval universities. Universities whose cultural development in general, or in certain special realms, was presumably lagging often invited scholars and scientists representing more advanced cultures. Thus, after the universities of Prague, Vienna, and Cracow were founded in the fourteenth century, they invited many Italian scholars. Russian universities and technical schools (founded in the eighteenth century and the first half of the nineteenth) were at first staffed mostly by French and German scientists and scholars, as the number of properly trained Russians was insufficient. European scientists and scholars contributed much to the development of American universities during their early period.

Such invitations continue to this day, even in the most advanced countries. When universities began to include curricula in foreign languages, literature, history, and art, foreigners familiar with these subjects were, and still are, considered best qualified to teach them. Indeed, in view of the vast wealth and complexity of knowledge and the rapidity of its growth by original contributions made by scientists and scholars of many nationalities, the culture of any nationality can be enriched by inviting foreign contributors to teach. This is what American universities quickly realized when, before and during World War II, "refugee scientists" were admitted to the United States and invited to function as teachers and investigators.

However, much more widely used is the method of promoting the growth of a national culture by including in universities and other centers of high education "native" leaders who have acquired superior learning in foreign centers. In the United States during the nineteenth century the teaching staff of most universities included young scientists and scholars who had completed their training in Europe—England, France, or (most frequently) Germany. When national universities were founded in Greece, Serbia, Rumania, Bulgaria, Lithuania, and Estonia, after these nationalities had gained independence, the staff was mostly composed of intellectuals previously trained abroad. When, after Poland regained independence, three new national universities were organized in addition to the old ones, and there were not enough scientists and scholars in Poland to fill the teaching positions, Poles who had been trained abroad and were teaching in foreign universities were invited—from Chicago in the West to Tomsk in the East, and from Stockholm in the North to Lisbon in the South. The foundation of national universities in Asia and the introduction of new subjects in Latin American universities were preceded by sending native teachers to be trained in Europe and the United States.

Ever since the seventeenth century, national scientific as-

150

sociations have usually welcomed or even invited foreigners to participate as visitors in meetings or to give lectures. More recently, prominent foreign scientists, scholars, and philosophers have been invited to become permanent members of national associations. This custom was, for instance, adopted by the American Philosophical Society, founded in Philadelphia at the end of the eighteenth century. Such foreign members are now commonly called "members-correspondents," as distinct from active members. This implies that between meetings, in which they are welcome to participate, the association maintains some intellectual contact with them through correspondence, but they are not full participants in its organization and have no influence whatever upon its collective functions. Some associations were reluctant to adopt this type of membership, but by now it has spread rather widely. In the twentieth century, every prominent thinker usually is, or has been, a member-correspondent of several foreign associations.

Very general is the admission of foreign musicians, singers, and conductors to temporary, sometimes permanent, participation in national groups—operatic companies, symphonic orchestras. The invitation of foreign soloists, however, to give concerts is often initiated not by professional musical associations, but by groups of amateurs and patrons of music. And patrons, rather than professional musicians, are usually the ones who invite a foreign musical group to play. In the past, this has sometimes provoked conflict. For instance, when groups of Italian singers and musicians began to be invited to play Italian operas in Berlin on the initiative of the royal court, this was opposed by German musicians and patriotic amateurs, and their opposition culminated in 1841 in a violent riot.[3] Later, however, not the musicians but nationalistic political groups as well as the public opposed the importation of foreign musicians, especially when the musicians or the composers whose works they played belonged to an "enemy" nationality. Thus, during World War I, after the United States joined the

3. Robert Michels, *Patriotismus*, p. 186.

Allies, German singers and musicians became *personae non gratae,* and German compositions and operas (especially Wagner's) were banned in most American cities. This hostile attitude soon changed, and few such bans occurred during World War II. But in Germany under the Nazi regime only German music was officially recognized as valuable.

Importation of foreign leaders in the domain of material culture began more than a century ago and continued for a long time. Technological planners and industrial managers from countries with highly developed material techniques were invited by powerful sponsors, political groups, and economic groups to promote the development of industries in countries where such techniques were less developed. Russian rulers, even after the Bolshevik Revolution, invited foreign technicians, though they certainly did not welcome foreign leaders in ideational culture.

However, in most technically backward countries foreign technologists were originally employed by the foreign capitalists who controlled the industries and allowed the natives to participate only as workers. Wherever a tendency to liberation from such control developed, native technicians were sent abroad to study engineering, so as to make their industry function under their own technical managers, even though economic management still remained in the hands of the foreign investors. Thus, it is probable that the majority of the foreign students who have come to the United States during the twentieth century have studied engineering.

The recent development of collective research in the domain of material techniques and the formation of organized groups devoted to such research by industrial corporations and governments have raised the demand for inventors and creative scientists. This demand is greatest in societies with a highly advanced technology. Consequently, we notice an unprecedented competition between such societies to attract scientists from countries where technical advancement is lagging or has been impeded. A

152

conspicuous example is the competition between the United States and Soviet Russia for German scientists, German technological development having practically stopped since the war.

Social groups tending to fertilize foreign national cultures

Tendencies of social groups to promote the creative growth of their own cultures are obviously more general than tendencies to stimulate the growth of other cultures, which presuppose a kind of collective "altruism" of relatively recent origin.

The beginning of such tendencies may be traced back to religious missions. Originally, most religious missionaries in foreign areas, while converting "unbelievers," tried to eliminate the "inferior" native culture and to substitute their own. This often provoked active resistance, especially when political or economic power was exerted. Missionaries had to face this problem for centuries and only slowly learned to solve it. They began to stimulate the development of native *secular* cultures by making the natives gradually acquainted with the creative growth of more developed cultures. They organized intellectual centers where not only religious, but secular, education was carried on, first under the guidance of cultural leaders imported from more advanced societies, later under the guidance of native leaders, either trained in these centers or abroad. On a lower educational level, this is exemplified by many missionary centers in Africa and, on a higher level, in Asia.

Such fertilization usually began in the applied sciences—medicine, agriculture, and engineering. With the partial secularization of the colleges and universities established by missions, other disciplines began to be taught. This is how Robert College, the University of Beirut, and especially Chinese universities became intellectual centers, transmitting the results of the work of Western cultural leaders to be used for the creative growth of the aboriginal cultures. In the Soviet Union, Russian intellectuals have been functioning both as missionaries converting to communism members of other nationalities and as cultural leaders stimulating the development of culturally backward ethnic groups (e.g., the Chuvash, Mordvinians, Uzbeks, Yakuts), not only in material techniques, but in literature, art, and science. Their efforts are comparable to those of American leaders from 1900 on to spread democratic ideals in the Philippines and also to promote the growth of Philippine culture.

The destruction brought by the two World Wars aroused the altruistic interest of certain groups which had not been subjected to such destruction. Their interest was primarily in alleviating the suffering of foreign peoples, but it resulted also in efforts to help them rebuild their material cultures, resume education of their young, and revive their cultural development. We may mention by way of example the work of the American Friends Service Committee, UNRRA,[4] the help given by American universities and libraries to reconstruct cultural centers destroyed by the Nazis, the assistance offered by various associations to professional people whose functions were impeded or interrupted during the war. The best known instance of such cultural fertilization is, of course, the promotion of technological and economic revival under the Marshall Plan.

Another well-known activity is stimulation of the development of agriculture in backward countries. This task, first undertaken by private "missions" of certain nationalities, became one of the functions of the International Agricultural Association, organized for mutual cooperation between several nationalities, and gained partial sponsorship of the League of Nations and full sponsorship of the United Nations. It is now connected with a plan for raising the educational level of the people in those countries.[5]

Sending prospective intellectual leaders of a nationality abroad to be trained in foreign educational centers has an ob-

4. Cf. UNRRA: *The History of the United Nations Relief and Rehabilitation Administration*, 3 vols., ed. George Woodbridge (New York: Columbia University Press, 1950).

5. Cf. Asher Hobson, *International Institute of Agriculture* (Berkeley: University of California Press, 1931); François Houillier, *L'Organisation internationale de l'agriculture* (Paris, 1935); John R. Scott, "International Food and Agricultural Organizations under the League of Nations and the United Nations" (manuscript). The significance of this function for mankind as a whole is well summarized by Frank H. Hankins, "Underdeveloped Areas with Special Reference to Population Problems," *International Social Science Bulletin*, II (1950), 307-16.

154

vious counterpart in the function of educating foreign students, which national universities and other intellectual centers have assumed. Of course, the original purpose of the latter was not to promote the development of foreign cultures, but to spread their own culture abroad and to raise the prestige and influence of their own nationality. The more foreign students a national university attracted, the greater its prestige and the further its culture spread. However, it was thought that learning should not be made too easy for foreigners, since this might lower the national prestige.

This function led to interesting competition between universities of different nationalities. For instance, in the seventeenth and eighteenth centuries French culture had much higher prestige abroad than German culture, and French educational centers attracted more foreigners. But in consequence of the development of German philosophy and science during the nineteenth century, the number of foreigners studying in German universities steadily increased. They were attracted also by the possibility of getting a doctor's degree there, whereas in France the requirements for such a degree were not only higher but could be satisfied only by those who had been educated in French secondary schools. However, when French intellectual leaders became fully aware of the effectiveness of German competition in attracting foreigners, a special doctor's degree was created which universities could grant to foreigners; it required much less preparation than the degree reserved for Frenchmen, and gave no status in the French system of higher education.[6]

In any case, universities at first manifested no interest in the native cultures of foreign students or in their future functions as leaders of their own nationalities. Only in recent times did such interest develop, due mainly to a growing realization that no nationality is completely self-sufficient in all realms of culture and that every one can benefit by having its future leaders learn something about the cultures of other nationalities and

6. Information about the new degrees is contained in a *Handbook for Foreigners*, published by the *Comité de patronage des étudiants étrangers* (Paris, 1902 and 1910).

155

7. Cf. *Bulletins of the Institute of International Education* (New York, started in 1920); *Bulletins of the International Bureau of Education* (Geneva, started in 1932); Stephen Duggan, *A Professor at Large* (New York: Macmillan, 1943); *Study Abroad; Fellowships, Scholarships, Educational Exchange* (Paris: UNESCO, 1948-51). A survey of the development of international exchange of university students was written by Tony Weiner (manuscript); of international exchange of teachers, by Dorothy Collins (manuscript); of international scholarships, by Eugene Jouglet (manuscript); of *Corda Fratres*, an association of cosmopolitan clubs of students and teachers, by Constance Rubin (manuscript).

8. Robert Doré, *Essai d'une bibliographie des congrès internationaux* (Paris, 1923). Goes back 50 years.

9. So far as we know, the earliest, outside of the natural sciences, was the International Congress of Anthropology and Prehistoric Archeology, which first met in Paris in 1863. The Congress of Orientalists started in Paris in 1873. The first Congress of Psychology met in Paris in 1890; the first Congress of Philosophy, also in Paris, met in 1900.

10. The growing differentiation of natural sciences is well

their creative contributions. As a result, during the last forty years associations have been gradually formed to promote and organize the *exchange* of students and teachers, at first between two nationalities, later between a particular nationality and several others, finally between every nationality and all the others.[7]

This is one type of international cooperation intended to promote not one-sided, but mutual, fertilization or cross-fertilization of national cultures. Another type, which began earlier and is much more developed, consists in a socially organized interchange of creative contributions between intellectual leaders of various nationalities.

International meetings of intellectual leaders

The earliest and best known associations intended to promote cultural cross-fertilization between nationalities are the international congresses during which scientists or scholars of several nationalities who specialize in the same realm of knowledge periodically meet, communicate the new results of their studies, and critically discuss them.[8] Such congresses seem to have been initiated first by small groups of specialists in the natural sciences—physics, astronomy, chemistry, biology, and medicine. They rapidly extended to other realms—ethnology, history, psychology, philosophy, economics, and sociology[9]— and with increasing specialization became further differentiated and multiplied.[10]

Each particular congress, of course, is a short-lasting association of the present participants; but eventually small committees are formed which function between congresses, publish reports of past meetings, and plan future meetings. And, although the contributions to an international congress are purely individual, yet national associations often sponsor the active participation of their members.

Inasmuch as an international congress meets in some city which is the cultural center (or one of the cultural centers) of a particular nationality, the association of scientists and scholars of this particular nationality assumes the task of arranging the meeting and inviting foreign visitors. It acts as host and gains thereby considerable prestige; indeed, national associations compete for this honor, and consequently successive international congresses meet in the cultural centers of different nationalities. Moreover, the national association which acts as host often succeeds in obtaining support from the local university, the government of the city where the meeting is held, even the government of the state, and in attracting attention from the press. This indicates that the function performed by international congresses of promoting the development of national cultures by making their leaders acquainted with the achievements of foreign leaders is recognized, however vaguely, by other institutionalized national groups and a part of the educated public.

In the realm of the fine arts, cultural cooperation began in the last quarter of the nineteenth century with exhibitions of new paintings and sculptures, produced by artists of various nationalities, and culminated in international congresses of artists, patrons, and connoisseurs, eight of which were held between the two wars. There have also been meetings of musicians of several nationalities, like those which the International Society for Contemporary Music has recently been arranging. Such meetings, like the international scientific congresses, are primarily intended to promote cultural interaction between specialists, but they also make the public acquainted with recent creative products of foreign artists and musicians.

We must also take into consideration the function of groups of dancers, like the famous Russian ballet, and of theatrical companies playing for foreign audiences, in promoting international understanding.

In the domain of material technique, analogous functions

exemplified in the realm of biology, where we find separate congresses of entomology, genetics, microbiology, etc. An attempt to counteract scientific specialization in general, not very successful, was started in Paris in 1935, when an International Congress for the Unity of Science met.

are performed by international fairs, or world fairs. Like the medieval fairs and the later national fairs, their primary task is to stimulate exchange of the diversified products in which producers in various areas specialize. By helping producers of every participating nationality to get into contact with consumers of other nationalities, and consumers of every nationality to become acquainted with products of other nationalities, and by giving merchants an opportunity to limit competition by voluntary agreements, a world fair is intended to promote economic cooperation between nationalities.

Gradually, however, the functions of international fairs have expanded on the initiative of leaders and associations tending to stimulate and popularize not only economic cooperation, but also mutual understanding and positive valuation between nationalities with different cultures. This tendency was most fully manifested at the New York World's Fair in 1939–40. Every nationality participating in the Fair had an opportunity to make the public at least superficially acquainted not only with samples of its technical products, but also with its creative achievements in art, music, literature, knowledge; its distinctive customs and mores; and its ethical and political ideals.

The same may be said of the meetings of sportsmen which have culminated in the Olympic Games.[11] Such popularization of foreign cultures is designed to appeal to the masses rather than to intellectual specialists. Although sport is indubitably culturally patterned and new varieties have developed in recent times, yet, after all, sport is essentially play, not culturally creative activity. International meetings of sportsmen imply competition, not cooperation, between individuals or teams from different nationalities; their significance lies in the fact that they stimulate a common, world-wide interest in the individual sportsmen and teams of many nationalities and make the public aware that all of them conform with the same ethical principles of fair play.

11. John Kieran, *The Story of the Olympic Games, 776 B.C.- 1936 A.D.* (New York: Stokes, 1936).

158

Permanent international associations

A very important step in the development of cultural co-operation between nationalities is the formation of lasting international associations for the solution of common problems.[12] The difference between this function and that of cultural fertilization is well exemplified by comparing an international medical congress for the mutual exchange of discoveries and inventions already made with the organization of individual physicians and medical groups of various nationalities initiated and sponsored by the Rockefeller Foundation for the cooperative solution of medical problems by new discoveries and inventions.[13]

The development of such cooperation, however, presupposes that the common problems do not involve any important ideological conflicts. No such conflicts existed until recently in the realm of medicine: the curing and preventing of disease was considered by physicians of all nationalities as their basic function, and this was to be exercised for the benefit of all men. Only when some German physicians under the Nazi regime declared that they had no such duties with respect to racially inferior human beings, did cooperation between them and the physicians of other nationalities become impossible. The saving of human lives in catastrophes, epidemics, and famines is almost universally approved. Even the duty of caring for the wounded soldiers in war, initiated by the founders of the Red Cross, has become accepted by most nationalities and is sponsored by most governments; consequently, an International Red Cross Committee and eventually a permanent international League of Red Cross Societies became organized.

In the domain of theoretic natural sciences, at first no ideological obstacles interfered with the cooperation of associations and institutions for the solution of common scientific problems. This is still true in astronomy.[14] In physics, chemistry, and biology most of the actual research is carried on by the

12. A good comparison of 36 such functionally differentiated associations, selected from more than 500, is Lyman White, *The Structure of Private International Organizations* (Philadelphia: Ferguson, 1933).

13. Helena Znaniecki Lopata, "International Cooperation in Medicine" (unpublished Master's thesis, University of Illinois, 1948). Now the World Health Organization, an agency of the United Nations, sponsors this cooperation.

14. The International Astronomical Union, formed in 1922, was revived in 1947, after an interruption of its functions during the war.

scientists within one nationality, but international associations of individual scientists and federations of national societies have been formed for such purposes as devising a common consistent terminology, integrating some of the results of past research, planning together some future research.[15] However, the technological application of certain results of physics and partly also of chemistry for destructive purposes in war has interfered with this cooperation or limited it to scientists of states connected by politico-military alliances.[16]

In the cultural sciences, international cooperation in research is successful only when it raises no controversial ideological issues, and it can be achieved more easily by organizing associations of those individual thinkers of various nationalities who avoid such controversies for the sake of a common goal than in forming federations of national associations. Rather instructive in this respect are the efforts of sociologists to cooperate on an international scale. The International Institute of Sociology, composed of individual sociologists from many nationalities, functioned effectively up to World War II, for its members shared the common goal of promoting the development of sociology as an objective science and having it recognized by the universities and academies of all nationalities. However much they might disagree individually as to the proper realm of sociology and the methods to be used, they tried to avoid controversial ethical and political issues.

After national sociological associations and institutes had been formed, an attempt was started to make the International Institute also a federation of these national groups; but some of the latter, having adopted definite nationalistic ideologies, were unwilling to join. After World War II, a new attempt to form a federation was made, and many national associations have joined it; [17] but since sociologists in communist-dominated countries have to accept the doctrine of Marxism-Leninism as absolutely true and are expected to use the results of sociological research exclusively for the realization of a communist

15. The limited functions of most of these associations are well exemplified in the realm of zoology: Richard Cooperment, "International Cooperation in Zoology" (manuscript).

16. Nevertheless, the International Union of Pure and Applied Chemistry, founded in 1876, is still very active; its sixteenth conference met in New York in September, 1951, and chemists from forty-two countries participated in it.

17. The International Sociological Association, formed at a conference in Oslo, September, 1949, held its first world congress in Zurich, September, 1950.

160

society, it is improbable that sociological associations in these countries will be allowed to cooperate with associations which do not accept this doctrine but continue to promote the growth of sociology as an objective science.[18]

Active international cooperation in historical research has been effective as regards ancient history. But cooperation between national associations in the realm of modern history, when their own nationalities are involved, is impeded by the difficulty of avoiding national prejudice and maintaining scientific objectivity.

As distinct from groups of individual philosophers (which we shall discuss later), national philosophic societies have found it almost impossible to cooperate in the solving of fundamental problems when these problems involve divergent philosophies of values.[19] Indeed, even in the ordinary course of international philosophic congresses, conflicts between national ideologists sometimes interfere with the normal mutual exchange of ideas. It is significant that logicians, who are not concerned with such controversial issues, decided in 1937 to have a separate international congress in Paris. When the first philosophic congress since the war was organized in Amsterdam in 1948, most of the philosophers in communist countries were not permitted by their governments to participate.[20]

We cannot discuss here in detail the difficulties which political scientists of different nationalities and juridical thinkers have to face in trying to develop common goals and plan methods by which they can be realized. We should emphasize, however, the difference between their functions and those of active statesmen. Cooperation between intellectual leaders in these realms began much earlier than cooperation between governments; for instance, some principles of international law were formulated by Grotius and other thinkers long before they were applied in practice.[21] Numerous political and juridical thinkers have been, and still are, cooperatively planning the organization and functions of the United Nations, continuing, de-

18. Cf. Florian Znaniecki, "European and American Sociology after Two World Wars," *Am. Jour. of Sociology*, Vol. XLI, No. 3 (November, 1950).

19. However, a bold attempt to form an International Institute of Philosophy was made in 1947 at a conference in Paris.

20. Notwithstanding all these difficulties, the number of international scientific associations (outside the Iron Curtain) has been steadily growing since World War II. Cf. *Directory of International Scientific Organizations* (Paris: UNESCO, 1950).

21. The first thorough historical study of these attempts was written by F. Laurent, in 18 volumes (Paris, 1850-79). Vols. I, II, and III were entitled *Histoire du droit des gens et des relations internationales*. Later, the title was changed to *Etudes sur l'histoire de l'humanité*; but, as the author stated in his preface to the second edition (1879), the subject has remained the same: "Le droit des gens . . . enseigne les lois qui régirent les peuples considérés comme membres de l'humanité."

22. Cf. Charles Dupuis, *Les An-técédents de la Société des Nations* (Hague: Academy of International Law, 1937).

veloping, and integrating the intellectual work of their predecessors who had planned the League of Nations and the earlier, more specialized, political and juridical international groups.[22] But the factual realization of this vast and complex ideational plan by the active cooperation of governments-in-power is continually being impeded by ideological conflicts concerning the "right" and the "wrong," and the methods which should be used.

However, ideological conflicts which interfere with inter-group cooperation for the solution of common problems do not necessarily preclude cultural cross-fertilization. Cultural groups of one nationality can select and use for the creative growth of their own culture only those products of other nationalities which seem valuable to them and ignore those which appear undesirable from the point of view of their ideology. Thus, some exchange of values and patterns in various realms of culture is still going on even between Western nationalities and those behind the Iron Curtain.

Organized economic cooperation between nationalities for the benefit of all of them has been rather slow to develop. It is generally recognized, indeed, by intellectual leaders that economic progress ultimately depends upon the utilization of nature by men, and not upon the exploitation of men by other men, and that the products of every society can contribute to the welfare of other societies. But the realization of these principles meets considerable obstacles, especially when the economic life of particular nationalities is controlled by separate sovereign states. The difficulty of promoting cooperation under these conditions is well exemplified by the present tendencies toward economic separatism in Western European countries and by the persistence of high tariffs imposed by most of them as well as by the United States on foreign goods.

Nevertheless, a few rather successful attempts have been made on a limited scale, sometimes on the initiative of private associations, more often under joint sponsorship of state gov-

162

ernments. Among private associations, we obviously cannot include international cartels, for these do not function on behalf of their nationalities, but on behalf of the corporations which participate in them, often to the detriment of the majority of people in their respective countries. Very different are the international federations of labor unions, trying to raise the economic status of workers in all countries and consequently to eliminate the use of cheap labor in competition between nationalities.[23] We should also take into consideration the cooperation between chambers of commerce of several nationalities.[24] The idea that economic agents should function in such a way as to promote the general welfare has been the explicit guiding principle of the International Federation of Rotary Clubs, though its factual influence is still rather weak. More important are such state-sponsored attempts to stimulate international cooperation as those initiated by the United States in relations with Latin American countries.[25] The work carried on recently under the sponsorship of the Economic and Social Council of the United Nations seems to be promising.

However, the only thorough, systematic development of continuous economic cooperation between a number of nationalities was initiated and carried on by the communist regime in the Soviet Union, and there is no doubt that it has been effective; but the methods used have aroused considerable conflict. To achieve such cooperation as rapidly as possible, centralized control of all production and distribution seemed necessary. Therefore, the development of industry and agriculture in every part of the Union was planned years ahead by a ruling group, and the realization of their plans in all realms, in the production as well as in the distribution of products, was controlled by centralized agencies. Partial decentralization was attempted from time to time, but this trend was always reversed. Inasmuch as plans were seldom fulfilled according to requirements, violence has been used to counteract all opposition and to repress all deviations of individuals or groups from the rules

23. These attempts started fifty years ago; cf. *Bibliographie de l'organisation internationale du travail* (Geneva, 1939). In 1921, they gained the sponsorship of the League of Nations; cf. F. G. Wilson, *Labor in the League System* (Stanford: Stanford University Press, 1936). During and immediately after the war, international labor conventions continued to meet in the United States and Canada. Right now, the Economic and Social Council of the United Nations has an International Labor Office, and an International Confederation of Free Labor Unions functions outside of Soviet Russia and her satellite countries.

24. An International Chamber of Commerce was organized in 1920-21. Cf. George L. Ridgeway, *Merchants of Peace* (New York: Columbia University Press, 1938).

25. Although at first mainly concerned with economics and political relations, this cooperation, as we know, became extended to all realms of culture. Cf. Carleton Beals, *Pan America* (Boston: Houghton, 1940); Duncan Aikman, *The All-American Front* (New York: Doubleday, 1941); ed. Ruth D. Masters, *Handbook of International Organizations in the Americas* (Washington: Carne-

gie Endowment for International Peace; see also publications of the Pan-American Union, Washington 6, D. C., 1945).

26. See, e.g., eds. Stuart Chase, Robert Dunn, and Rexford G. Tugwell, *Soviet Russia in the Second Decade* (New York: Day, 1928); A. Yugoff, *Economic Trends in Soviet Russia,* trans. by E. and C. Paul (London, 1930); William H. Chamberlain, *The Russian Enigma* (New York: Scribner, 1944); Maurice Dobb, *Soviet Economic Development since 1917* (London, 1949).

27. See Ygael Sluckstein, *Stalin's Satellites in Europe. Operation Plunder* (New York: Beacon Press, 1952).

laid down by the supreme authorities. Consequently, just as in early periods of industrial capitalism, ethical standards of humanitarianism were subordinated to economic standards of technical efficiency.[26]

Moreover, since World War II the Bolshevik rulers have attempted to make the nationalities in satellite countries participate in the system of economic cooperation which has developed within the Soviet Union. Since these rulers are mostly Russians and the Russian nationality dominates all the others, this cooperation is organized in such a way as to benefit the republic of Soviet Russia proper rather than its satellites. It begins to follow the old model of economic exploitation of subjugated colonial peoples by the ruling nationality.[27]

Thus, the Soviet experiment has left unsolved a fundamental problem: economic planning being indispensable for long-term economic cooperation between nationalities, how can they make plans by mutual agreement and how can they realize them by *voluntary efforts?*

Popularization of international cooperation

All the types of social cooperation between nationalities mentioned above, just like the social unification of any nationality, were initiated by intellectual leaders and carried on by groups of intellectuals. And they were also followed by organized attempts to popularize international cooperation through propaganda and education. The general tendency is to overcome antagonistic national prejudices by substituting positive mutual valuations. This is done, first, by having people realize that foreigners are essentially human like themselves and should be treated as such; second, by making them understand and appreciate foreign cultures different from their own.

The first, humanitarian, conception goes back to the world religions, each including peoples of widely different traditional

164

and national cultures; its application was, of course, often impeded by the efforts of certain believers to convert unbelievers to their own religion, which resulted in conflict between religious groups. However, some such conflicts have recently been eliminated, and the humanitarian principle is consistently applied by certain religious or semi-religious groups acting not only without ethnic, but without religious, discrimination. We have mentioned the Quakers (American Friends Service Committee), who are working for peoples of different nationalities and different religions without trying to convert them. Much better known, more inclusive, and widely spread are the humanitarian functions of the YMCA and the YWCA.

Several secular international associations are now promulgating this ideal. Associations of youths under the guidance of adults are trying to impart it to the young generation by appealing to the common interests of the youth of all nationalities, exchanging information about their activities, helping small groups of young people to travel abroad, guiding them, and arranging intergroup meetings.[28] Quite a few schools have encouraged correspondence of their pupils with pupils of foreign schools.

Appreciation of the diversity of cultures was initiated in the eighteenth century by some philosophers of history, especially Herder, according to whom every culture is valuable because it enriches the total cultural life of mankind. The idea spread, though slowly, mostly under the influence of ethnologists positively interested in the cultures they study and try to understand without prejudice. Gradually it became popularized.

An active manifestation of this idea is the attempt of cultural leaders of some nationalities to revive folk cultures and tribal cultures which have been disappearing under the impact of modern national cultures. Of course, not all of their components can be revived: modern science, technology, and social organization have definitely eliminated most of the early be-

28. Here belong, for instance, the various international amateur athletic associations which include young people, the International Federation of Youth Hostels, international camps, the International Bureau of Boy Scouts, the World Bureau for Girl Guides and Girl Scouts: Stanford C. Kaatz, "International Youth Organizations" (manuscript).

liefs and patterns of actions. The revivals are for the most part limited to art, music, poetry, certain customs and mores, patterns of clothes, food, and drink. The popularization of such revivals was at first planned to make people of the same nationality living in different regions acquainted with the original diversity of their folk cultures. Eventually, however, acquaintance with the traditional cultures of peoples not belonging to the same nationality was promoted. This is well exemplified in the United States, where acquaintance of Americans with various immigrant folk cultures and tribal Indian cultures, as well as mutual acquaintance of immigrants with their different folk cultures is stimulated during interethnic festivals and in the course of travels.

Travel, to be sure, is the oldest and best-known method of becoming at least superficially acquainted with foreign cultures. But such superficial acquaintance does not always promote a positive valuation of those cultures. Far from it. When we read descriptions by travelers of their experiences and observations, we notice that, unless they originally aimed to understand and appreciate other cultures, negative rather than positive valuations of foreigners prevail. Modern tourists traveling rapidly and stopping briefly in foreign countries about which they know little frequently manifest negative prejudices, which are reciprocated by the attitudes of aborigines toward tourists. Gradually, however, many organized groups began to work purposefully to make tourism contribute toward mutual understanding and positive appreciation of foreigners and their cultures. On the one hand, groups which want to attract tourists, whether for economic reasons or to promote national prestige, planfully try to make travel as attractive as possible to foreign visitors and to guide them in such a way as to acquaint them with only the best cultural products and patterns of the country which they are visiting. This was perhaps best exemplified by the treatment and guidance of foreign tourists in Soviet Russia before World War II. On the other hand, groups of tourists are being organized under the guidance of competent leaders who try to make their travels not only satisfactory, but also instructive, by helping them become acquainted with the most important components of foreign cultures and learn to understand and appreciate them as well as can be done during the brief periods at their disposal.

We should not neglect the contribution of the press, especially of foreign correspondents, to mutual cultural appreciation. To obtain interesting information from foreign peoples, a correspondent must manifest some degree of sympathetic understanding of their life and culture; and, although not everything he learns and reports is favorable to them, yet he can continue to function effectively as long as his published reports are considered relatively friendly by the foreign groups. Of course, his task is more difficult if there are strong conflicts within the foreign collectivity; he is then faced with the problem whether he should take sides or remain impartial. The world-wide popularity of the *National Geographic Magazine* is due not only to the considerable scientific knowledge which it popularizes, but also to the fact that articles describing human collectivities in various geographic areas include only positive evaluative judgments about those collectivities; and conflicts are carefully omitted or soft-pedalled.

Teaching young people to understand and appreciate foreign cultures is not so easy. In recent times, some popularized knowledge of particular cultures and of the peoples who share them has been imparted in schools, especially American schools.[29] However, negative prejudice against foreigners is not one sided, but many sided, and can be effectively counteracted only by continuous cooperation between the schools of various nationalities for the purpose of spreading mutual understanding.[30]

Within the Soviet Union and lately between Russia and her satellite countries such educational cooperation has been developing, but much more emphasis is put on making the youth

29. See, e.g., William E. Vickary and Steward G. Cole, *International Education in American Schools* (New York: Harper, 1947).

30. Many plans to promote such understanding have been developed; some include the programs for exchange of students and teachers mentioned above, though mostly on the primary and secondary school level. Cf. William George Carr, *Education for World Citizenship* (Stanford: Stanford University Press, 1928); John Eugene Harley, *International Understanding: Education for a New World* (Stanford: Stanford University Press, 1931); *International Understanding through Youth* (Paris: League of Nations, International Institute of Intellectual Cooperation, 1933); Ben Mark Cherrington, *Methods of Education in International Attitudes* (New York: Columbia University Press, 1934); *Working Papers of the Seminar of Education for International Understanding* (Paris, 1947).

of other nationalities appreciate Russian culture than on having the Russian youth appreciate the other cultures. And, obviously, right now the main obstacle to mutual understanding between nationalities within the Soviet sphere and the rest of the world is the continuous indoctrination by the communist regimes of whole populations, who are being taught to evaluate *negatively* the social life and cultures of the capitalist countries.

While popularization of the understanding and appreciation of other nationalities and their cultures imparts to individuals positive attitudes toward foreigners and eliminates or weakens negative attitudes, it does not contribute directly to *active* international cooperation—obviously not when those who learn about foreigners never get into direct contact with them. Some social leaders, especially in the United States, have stimulated such cooperation on a small scale in areas where immigrants of different nationalities and their descendants live in relative proximity; here organized groups composed of people of various cultures are formed for the realization of specific common purposes. An extension of such cooperation to the large masses of people living in distant areas meets well-known practical obstacles. However, when during the war and the subsequent occupation large numbers of soldiers and military technicians, especially Americans, came into contact with foreign civilian populations, they were usually given in advance a minimum of information about certain important components of the cultures of these populations, so as to prevent any misunderstandings which might result in conflict. And some of them, who were expected to function as leaders or mediators, learned enough about these cultures to promote active cooperation. Although nonetheless many conflicts did occur, yet some of the American soldiers on returning home brought with them considerable understanding and appreciation of culturally different nationalities; and many of the people with whom the soldiers had been in contact learned to understand and appreciate the American nationality as never before.

Anyway, though the majority of the people of any nationality have no opportunity to participate actively in social groups organized for international cooperation, yet the spread of positive appreciation of foreign cultures and peoples through education and propaganda has considerable influence on *public opinion* and thus wins the general approval of international cooperation. The prevalent acceptance of the Good Neighbor Policy and the Marshall Plan by the American public, the enthusiastic support of the efforts of UNESCO in many American communities are significant instances.

The function of political societies in promoting cultural cooperation

All types of cultural cooperation between nationalities have been in some measure conditioned by governmental organizations of political societies and by relations between them. A government can promote, impede, or ignore intergroup cultural cooperation within its boundaries. We have seen how the Bolshevik government has been promoting cooperation between the national culture societies within the Soviet Union. When a state government serves the aggressive expansion of the dominant culture society at the cost of another culture society whose members are subjected to its rule—as the Tsarist government did in Russia or the Hohenzollern government in Prussia during the last quarter of the nineteenth century—this makes active cooperation between those societies impossible. In other cases, e.g., in Great Britain and Canada, during the twentieth century the state, while trying to prevent conflicts between the cultural societies within its borders, leaves the matter of cooperation between them to their own initiative.

In those relations between national culture societies which cut across state boundaries, effective cooperation between them

169

is obviously helped by interstate cooperation and impeded by interstate conflicts. We have seen how much economic cooperation depends upon the political relations between governments. Cooperation between states in such matters as communication and transportation is an essential condition of active cooperation between culture societies, though heretofore it has oftener been instrumental in their aggressive expansion, especially economic. Every kind of interstate cooperation for peaceful settlement of political conflicts is a step toward cultural cooperation. And insofar as the voluntary initiative of cultural leaders of different nationalities in organizing groups for the solution of common problems and for the pursuit of common goals succeeds in gaining the sponsorship of governments, it brings quicker results. This is exemplified by the Red Cross, by the various cooperative organizations (the Committees on International Communication and Transit, Economics and Finance, Health, Labor) which worked under the sponsorship of the League of Nations (disbanded in 1946); and by those much more numerous organizations which are now sponsored by the Economic and Social Council of the United Nations, and especially by UNESCO.

However, it is surprising how limited this sponsorship has been and how rare the initiative of state governments in matters of cooperation between national-culture societies, especially in view of the vast possibilities which the creative expansion of national cultures opens for common constructive work.[31] Only a small proportion of "private" international associations was sponsored by the League of Nations, and some of those which it did sponsor gained very little help. Thus, the Committee for Intellectual Cooperation was for the most part limited to collecting and publishing information about what private intellectual associations were doing, and obtaining nominal approval of their activities by the League as a political body.

31. For a brief outline of some governmental attempts to initiate international cultural cooperation, see Ruth E. McMurry and Muna Lee, *The Cultural Approach* (Chapel Hill: University of North Carolina Press, 1947).

170

Probably the chief factor of this limitation is the tendency of every state to maintain its sovereignty in relation to other states and its supreme control over all other kinds of social groups within its borders. A government has seldom sponsored movements which, by promoting cultural bonds and social co-operation between its people and peoples belonging to other political societies might interfere with the sovereign freedom of its state to remain politically isolated or to carry on active conflicts with other states. Very instructive in this respect is the case of the Red Cross, which governments agreed to sponsor only under the condition that it would not become an organization acting for the promotion of international peace.

How unwilling governments are to grant the power of co-operative action to any large group which they cannot fully and authoritatively control is shown by the careful way in which the Constitution of the League of Nations was framed so as to prevent it from becoming anything more than a league of sovereign states. Thus, although it tried to protect "minorities" within states when their cause was sponsored by some state, it refused even to acknowledge the corporate existence of nationality groups as such or to grant them any right to appeal directly to the committee dealing with "minority problems." [32] And it did nothing to promote large-scale international studies of the relationships between nationalities or cooperative planning by competent scientists, which might have weakened or delayed the world crisis.

The United Nations is certainly much more active and much more conscious of the importance of conflict and cooperation between nationalities as cultural collectivities. The difference between it and the League of Nations is well exemplified by the number and diversity of international associations which it sponsors.[33] Still, the funds at its disposal are inadequate for efficient sponsorship, and it often meets considerable resistance to its plans from particular governments—not only those con-

32. The very term "minority" did not mean a distinct and separate nationality group whose members formed a minority within a state whose majority was composed of members of another nationality, but a minority of members of a "nation" (in the sense of a sovereign state) who differed in some respect—religion, language, race—from the majority of members of the same "nation" ($=$ state). Cf. Joseph S. Roucek, *The Working of the Minorities System under the League of Nations* (Prague, 1929).

33. Over one hundred by the end of 1949. However, the United Nations, as was the League of Nations, is still handicapped by the fact that it is an *intergovernmental* organization: Jean Gasaway (manuscript). The limitations of its functions are definitely stated in the "Text of Directives concerning UNESCO's Relations with International Non-governmental Organizations," *International Social Science Bulletin*, Vol. II, No. 4 (1950).

34. Cf. Robert C. Angell, "So-ciology and the World Crisis," presidential address at the meeting of the American Soci-ological Society, 1951. This meeting was primarily devoted to the problem of "Sociology and the World Order."

trolled by communists. And though it did promote some scientific study of the conflicts between nationalities and is beginning to promote studies of cooperation, it will be a long time before these studies become sufficiently broad, inclusive, and methodical for efficient planning of a culturally harmonious world.[34]

seven

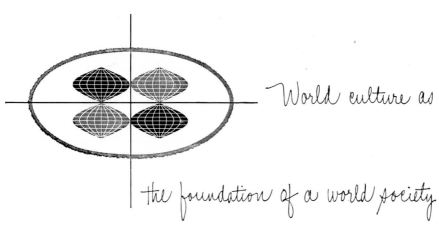

World culture as

the foundation of a world society

Philosophic conceptions of world unity

The ideal of a politically united world, a "cosmopolis," was explicitly formulated by the Stoics. But it was preceded and influenced by the Platonic conception of one universal system of supreme values—intellectual, ethical, and aesthetic—in which all men could participate to some degree, if adequately prepared. This system was presumably discovered by men, though not created by men. It was supposed to exist by itself, as an impersonal system of pure ideas, or in the absolute Mind of God. The ideal of a united world society could be fully realized, if mankind under the guidance of intellectual leaders and social rulers learned to accept this system and to conform with its basic principles of Truth, Goodness, and Beauty.

For two thousand years, efforts were made to achieve world unity based on such a system of supreme values. Many Roman political and intellectual leaders, influenced by the Stoical ideal, expected Rome to unify the world under universal principles of peace, order, and justice. Thus, Cicero emphasized the need of maintaining and spreading these principles, already included in the Roman political order, and did his best as ethical and legal leader to prevent the deterioration of this order. So did some of the emperors—e.g., Antoninus Pius and Marcus Aurelius.

After the emergence of Christianity, the Roman Catholic Church claimed to be the bearer of supreme universal values and assumed the task of unifying all mankind spiritually. It needed, however, the help of a state to achieve political unification and therefore tried to resurrect the Roman ideal of a world empire, but under the condition that its builders and rulers should submit to the intellectual guidance of religious authorities.

The failure of the Church to prevent violent political conflicts, even within Western Europe, the ceaseless struggles between Christians and Moslems, and especially the occurrence

174

of religious wars between Christian groups after the Protestant Reformation, led Western secular thinkers to substitute different conceptions of a future world unity, which were based upon generalizations derived from the past history of mankind. However these conceptions might differ otherwise, they all included the expectation that the future course of human history would result in a common secular culture, a "civilization," and a world-wide politically united society. This expectation was expressed by famous philosophers of the eighteenth and nineteenth centuries, e.g., Kant, Condorcet, Hegel, Comte, Marx and Engels, Spencer.[1]

Whether, according to those thinkers of the past, political unity was supposed to come first and cultural unity later, or cultural unity had to precede political unity, all of them assumed that common cultural or, more specifically, ideational bonds are an essential condition without which no united society can exist. In the light of a comparative study of human societies and of their relationships, we must agree with this assumption. But it raises the problem: Are there enough cultural bonds common to all mankind to make a lasting world society possible?

At first glance, the answer seems to be negative. There certainly is no common system of religious values. All attempts to integrate the numerous and diverse religious ideologies have failed—at best, they have helped to reduce somewhat the conflicts between religious groups. Differences between national cultures are irreducible: although cooperation between nationalities is apparently increasing and conflict decreasing, this does not mean that their cultures can be united. While the communist ideological system is now shared by a larger proportion of mankind than any other system ever was, not only does it conflict with other ideologies, religious and secular, but even within its own range many cultural conflicts emerge, though they are temporarily prevented by force from resulting in political conflict.

1. For a good historical survey of ideals of world unity from 1300 to 1889, see Jacob ter Meulen, *Der Gedanke der internationalen Organisation in seiner Entwicklung*, 3 vols. (Hague, 1917-40).

And yet during the last hundred years a new conception of a world culture to be shared by all mankind has been developed by intellectual leaders. According to this conception, a world culture (unlike sacred cultures, as conceived by ecclesiastical thinkers) is not yet ready and completed—and never will be. It is being slowly created and will continue to be created indefinitely. Its creation does not mean elimination of the present diversity of cultures, for it cannot be created out of nothing: it grows and is expected to grow out of national cultures, just as national cultures grew out of older cultures—but with a difference. Whereas those older cultures were relatively static and hence became partly or entirely supplanted by national cultures as the latter developed and expanded, national cultures are dynamic, and it is their continual creative growth which makes the emergence and growth of a "supernational" world culture possible.

Appreciation and preservation of the common cultural heritage of mankind

The conception of a world culture includes both past achievements and future potentialities. According to many modern historians of culture and philosophers of history, the most original and valuable cultural products of the past, no matter by whom they were produced or how much they differ, are common possessions of humanity and as such should be preserved and made generally accessible to all mankind. This idea has been applied to the fine arts, music, literature, religion, and philosophy.

Preservation of works of art—architecture, sculpture, painting—is now generally recognized as important, because they are valuable not only to historians, but to present and future artists, students, amateurs, and the public at large. For new, original, and valuable creative achievements require a knowledge of past achievements, and some understanding and appreciation of the fine arts is an essential part of the cultural education of every individual. Recognition of the importance to all mankind of the best artistic works of the past, wherever produced, is most obviously manifested in the maintenance and development of the museums which include products and reproductions of Greek, Roman, and Egyptian art; the art of Western Asia, India, and China; European art from the Dark Ages down to modern times. This recognition is expressed in numerous popular histories of art, textbooks, and courses in the general history of culture. It was explicitly shown during World War II, when British and American airmen were told to avoid bombing artistically valuable buildings and museums in enemy cities and when even the collections of paintings hidden by the Nazis were saved from destruction.[2]

2. Patricia Collins, "Protection of Artistic Works during World War II" (manuscript).

In the realm of music, the products of composers which have gained universal fame are played wherever professional musicians perform. It matters not to what nationality the composer belonged: what is essential is that his works are judged highly valuable by musicians and audiences of all nationalities, and that musicologists and historians consider them as important contributions to music in general.

Renaissance thinkers developed the idea that prominent works of aesthetic literature, as common hereditary possessions of humanity, should be perpetuated and made forever accessible to readers. It was applied at first only to classical Greek and Latin literature, but was later extended to Oriental and Western national literatures. However, there is an obvious difficulty in making these works generally accessible. A literary work, unlike a work of plastic art or music, can be understood only by those who know its language, and nobody can know all the multiple and diverse literary languages in which aesthetically valuable works have been written.

Indeed, linguistic differences have always been a considerable obstacle in the way of mutual understanding. Some intellectual leaders tried to overcome this obstacle by inventing and popularizing a new world language including components of many existing languages—e.g., Volapük and Esperanto—that could be learned and used by peoples of all nationalities. Others attempted to have an existing language universally accepted in a more or less simplified form—e.g., modernized Latin or Basic English.[3] Probably sooner or later some common system of verbal symbols will come into use to facilitate communication between nationalities, but it will certainly not be a substitute for national languages, whose uniqueness enhances the originality of their creative works, past, present, and future.

As a matter of fact, even without a common world language, prominent literary works, in whatever language they were written, are being made increasingly accessible to people of many nationalities by translations. Such translations show that these works have actually become common values to numerous readers all over the world and are already recognized as integral components of the cultural heritage which all of them share. The General Assembly of the United Nations has planned to strengthen common cultural bonds between nationalities by organizing an international committee that would select works judged to be "classics," promote their translation, and have their reading generally accepted as a part of advanced education.[4]

This recognition of important creative works of the past as lasting contributions to the total growth of human culture has been extended to religion and philosophy. The underlying principle is that, however much disagreement there may be between various religious doctrines and between divergent philosophical theories, many of them have added something original and significant to human thinking, and that present thinkers of all nationalities should learn to understand and appreciate their positive contributions. Such is, for instance, the purpose of the program of college education based on "great books," intended to make students acquainted with the best

3. Cf., e.g., Léon Guénard, A Short History of the International Language Movement (London, 1922); Charles K. Ogden, Basic English versus the Artificial Languages (London, 1935); Herbert N. Shenton, Cosmopolitan Conversation (New York: Columbia University Press, 1933).

4. A. Wojcicki, "Working Paper on the Problem of World Classics," 1947. (Mimeographed.)

results of human thought and help them realize that ideological differences do not necessarily involve social conflicts.[5]

This exaltation of universal cultural history has the same function, on a broader scale, as exaltation of national history. It is supposed to develop, and actually does develop, consciousness of a rich and valuable world heritage of ideational culture which all men share and which should be accepted as a common bond uniting humanity. Such is the leading purpose of the International Committee formed by the UNESCO in Paris which plans to prepare and publish a "Scientific and Cultural History of Mankind."

As yet this consciousness is limited to a small minority of people, since sharing the most important components of the cultural heritage of mankind requires education on a higher level than sharing the main products of a particular national culture. Nonetheless, remembering how education in national cultural history has slowly, but steadily, expanded, we may expect a similar expansion of education in the cultural history of the world.

Ideals of further cultural progress of humanity

However, while sharing common cultural products of the past makes people conscious of belonging to the society which produced them, it is not enough by itself to stimulate and maintain active social solidarity. Therefore, just as national leaders promulgated ideals of the future development of their nationalities and initiated organized cooperation for the realization of these ideals, leaders tending to promote world unity are promulgating ideals of the *future* development and trying to have their ideals realized.

These ideals are derived from the last century's general ideal of universal human progress. Now, "progress" is an evaluative concept. It means continual "improvement," a sequence

5. Cf., e.g., the list of "Great Books" in Mortimer Adler, *How to Read a Book* (New York: Simon & Schuster, 1940).

179

of changes from one period to the next, in the course of which every subsequent period becomes more valuable than the preceding one. Thus, it implies some standards of valuation by which the results of those changes can be judged.

With the exception of a few thinkers who believe that the course of human history is determined in advance by divine will or by some metaphysical essence of the universe, ideologists of a future world society are well aware that human progress can be achieved only by cooperation of human agents. Such cooperation obviously requires, first of all, acceptance of a common *philosophy of values,* enabling agents to agree as to what constitutes progress, what changes already achieved are valuable, and what new changes are desirable and ought to be achieved in the future. Second, it requires the use of *effective methods* for the preservation of valuable results of past activities and for the realization of desirable results by future activities.

Now, such a philosophy of values already exists and is rather widely accepted. It is based on the ethical principle that men in general, wherever they live, to whatever societies they belong, irrespective of differences in age, sex, race, and class, should always be considered and treated by other men as highly important positive values.

This principle was formulated long ago by famous religious prophets and is shared by many religious thinkers, although in most religions divine beings, as conceived by their worshipers, are regarded as incomparably more valuable than human beings. The same principle has been proclaimed in modern times by semi-secular and secular thinkers throughout the world and has been accepted by their followers. It is considered the fundamental ethical principle of Western democracy, as well as of communism, according to its adherents; it is also recognized as universally binding by modern intellectual leaders in India. It is explicitly contained in the programs of numerous and diverse international associations and has been expressed in declarations of several committees of the United Nations.[6]

In accordance with this principle, the ideal of human progress includes: steady, universal improvement of human health; technological advancement raising the level of human welfare throughout the world; full intellectual, moral, and aesthetic development of human personalities through education; gradual functional integration of all the powerful social groups into one well-ordered world society; continuous collective promotion of creativeness in every realm of culture.

There does not seem to be much disagreement between intellectual leaders as to these ideals. But when it comes to the methods by which they are to be realized, not only disagreements, but conflicts, are so strong that their realization appears doubtful.

Of course, it is generally recognized that the realization of the first two ideals—improvement of human health and increase of human welfare—requires continuous creative growth of scientific knowledge about nature by new discoveries and new theories and its practical applications by new inventions. Indeed, some optimistic thinkers of the nineteenth century assumed that the progress of natural sciences and of their practical application was not only a necessary, but a sufficient, condition of human progress in general. Such optimism has been badly shaken since the results of natural sciences have been more and more widely and effectively applied for the purpose of *destroying* human lives and the products of material culture. This does not imply that the scientists who use knowledge for this purpose reject the ideal of human progress; in fact, most of them sincerely believe that such applications of science, though undesirable, are indispensable to counteract other destructive forces which threaten the future of mankind. The root of this belief lies in the conviction that the basic ethical principle according to which men are important positive values and should be treated as such is inapplicable to those men whose conduct conflicts with it, who manifest negative

6. The Commission on Human Rights accepts the principle, but has considerable difficulty in getting it applied in legal enactments by the participating governments. For what it would mean, if generally applied, see Hersh Lauterpacht, *The International Bill of Human Rights* (New York: Columbia University Press, 1945); and Georges Gurvitch, *The Bill of Social Rights* (New York: International Universities Press, 1946).

attitudes toward others, and whose actions are harmful to others. These men are "bad," and in the interest of "good" men they should by force be made incapable of doing harm.

This age-old conviction underlies the treatment of harmful individuals as "criminals" who have to be incapacitated by such methods as death, banishment, imprisonment, deprivation of all means by which harm might be inflicted. It is also manifested in violent struggles between exclusive, self-centered collectivities: once such a struggle has started, each collectivity tries to justify it by asserting the badness of its enemies, who are doing harm or intend to do harm to its own good people and consequently must be incapacitated by the use of violence—destroyed, disorganized, subjected to effective coercive control, etc.

It has been extended in recent times to all kinds of individuals and groups whose conduct, according to those who judge it, is harmful to mankind in general and consequently must be repressed by force for the benefit of humanity. For instance, according to absolutely righteous communists, all capitalists are exploiters of the working people and have to be eliminated or at least deprived of their possessions by force; and all individuals and groups who impede the advancement of communism are "enemies of the people" and must be forcibly destroyed or at least incapacitated. On the other hand, according to the judgment of absolutely righteous opponents, all communists are dangerous enemies of human freedom, happiness, and progress in general, and force is the only effective method of getting rid of them.

It is astonishing that these generalizations, according to which men can be divided into two classes—"good" and "bad" —and violent coercion is the only efficient method of preventing "bad" men from doing harm to "good" men, are still so widely accepted and applied in practice in our age, although neither of them has any scientific foundation, and at a time when all generalizations concerning nature are based on objective scientific research and their practical applications scientifically tested.

Most of the leading ideologists striving to promote the progress of mankind are well aware that such progress is possible only if scientific knowledge, theoretic and applied, about human individuals, collectivities, and cultures is substituted for primitive popular assumptions, just as scientific knowledge about natural phenomena has been substituted for primitive assumptions permeated with mythical ontology and magic. We observe, therefore, that continual advancement of human psychology, sociology, and cultural sciences in general is considered by prominent thinkers as essential for the realization of the three ideals previously mentioned: the full development of human personalities which will make every individual valuable, the development of a functionally united world society, and the illimited creative growth of culture by cooperation.

As we noticed in the preceding chapter, it is often difficult to achieve cooperation between national associations in such realms of knowledge as history, sociology, political science, and economics. These difficulties are mostly due to lack of scientific objectivity. As long as some groups of scholars and scientists manifest favorable, others unfavorable, biases toward the peoples, the cultures, and the social systems which they study, no agreement between them is possible.

However, during the last fifty years many scientists of various nationalities have come to the conclusion that scientific objectivity in studies of social life and culture, just as in studies of nature, makes the results of such studies not only more productive and valid theoretically, but more useful practically. And it does not matter to what society these scientists belong: the agglomerated results of their research contribute to the creative growth of the total human knowledge about human individuals, collectivities, and cultures. The main obstacle right now is the attempt of many ruling groups—especially communist regimes—to make the peoples whom they rule, and their cultures, inaccessible to objective scientific research. But this obstacle is not insuperable; a considerable amount of at least hypothetically valid knowledge is being gathered and eventually will be tested.

We shall realize the importance of this advancement of the sociocultural sciences when we compare the functions of the intellectual leaders trying to develop a world culture and world unity with those of the intellectual leaders who developed national cultures and national unity. The problems which world leaders are facing in the present are similar to those which national leaders faced in the past. How to spread among the masses the consciousness of belonging to the same society? How to make the ideals of future progress generally understood and accepted? How to overcome ethnic separatism? How to reduce or eliminate political conflicts, class conflicts, conflicts between believers in the absolute truth of divergent dogmas?

In some instances, it took leaders of particular nationalities several centuries, never less than one century, to reach solutions of these problems sufficient for the formation of a solidary, permanent society united by a creatively growing culture. This process was slow at first, chiefly because, at the time when national cultures began to emerge, objective scientific knowledge about human personalities, collectivities, and cultures did not yet exist. Consequently, in attempting to solve their problems, national leaders had to use trial-and-error methods instead of the methods of applied science.

The increasingly rapid development of sociocultural sciences during the last hundred years offers intellectual world leaders a definite advantage. Unfortunately, many powerful politicians and dogmatic doctrinaires are scientifically ignorant and usually unaware of their ignorance. But this is an old difficulty which thinkers applying the results of theoretic science to practical purposes have always met and sooner or later succeeded in overcoming. There are hopeful signs that they are beginning to do so.[7]

7. Cf. Florian Znaniecki, *Cultural Sciences* (Urbana: University of Illinois Press, 1952), Chap. 15.

184

index

I. Index to Subjects[1]

Academies: literary, 60-63; scientific, 62-64

Africa, 24, 119, 153

Alsace-Lorraine, 129

American Friends Service Committee; *see* Quakers

Art: folk, 46-47; national, 45-50; religious, 46-47

Artists: international cooperation of, 149, 151, 157; patronized by rulers, 58-59

Asia, 23-24, 150, 153

Assimilation: in areas with a mixed population, 128-30; of foreign immigrants, 130-31; and racial prejudice, 127-31; and subordinate nationalities, 131-32

Associations: international, 159-65; national, 61-66; *see also* Social groups

Australia, 119

Austria, 42, 76, 102, 105, 117, 128, 131

Balkans, 117

Ballet, 157

Bavaria, 58

Berlin, 62-63

Bohemia; *see* Nationalities—Czechish

Bolsheviks; *see* Nationalities—Russian

Brandenburg, 117

British Colonial Empire; *see* Great Britain

Byzantine Empire, 42

Byzantium, 46

Capitalists, 53-56, 98, 102, 124, 164, 169, 182; *see also* Communism; Conflicts; Nationalities—Russian

Catholics; *see* Roman Catholic Church

Caucasus, 118

Central America, 37

Christians, 98, 102, 116, 127

Churches; *see* Greek Orthodox Church; Roman Catholic Church; Protestants

Cities, centers of cultural leaders, 59-60

Citizenship, xiii-xiv

Collectivities, ix-xiv; organized, 5-7, 15-29

Colonization; *see* Expansion of national culture societies; Immigrants

Common descent, 86-93

Communication, symbolic, 7-10

Communism; *see* Nationalities—Russian

Conflicts: class, 38; between nationalities, 113-41; political, 36; prevention of, 139-41; religious, 37-38, 40-41, 174

Congresses, international, of scientists and scholars, 161

Cooperation: defensive, 143-44; cultural, 144-53; interindividual, 146-47; of social groups, 141, 148-53; *see also* Fertilization; Cross-fertilization of cultures

Constantinople, 117

Corsica, 109

Courts, as social centers for cultural leaders, 58

Cracow, 63, 149

Crimea, 118, 138

Cross-fertilization of cultures, 145-52, 162

Cult of heroes; *see* Heroes

Culture: components of, ideational and material products of human actions, 2-4; and patterns of human actions, 4-5; definition of, 1-15; world, 15, 174-84 *passim*

[1] Most countries and peoples mentioned in the text are listed under Nationalities.

II. Index to Names